THE <u>CORPORATION</u> BUS

Ken Houston

Grosvenor House
Publishing Limited

All rights reserved
Copyright © Ken Houston, 2010

Ken Houston is hereby identified as author of this
work in accordance with Section 77 of the Copyright, Designs
and Patents Act 1988

The book cover picture is copyright to Ken Houston

This book is published by
Grosvenor House Publishing Ltd
28-30 High Street, Guildford, Surrey, GU1 3HY.
www.grosvenorhousepublishing.co.uk

This book is sold subject to the conditions that it shall not, by way of
trade or otherwise, be lent, resold, hired out or otherwise circulated
without the author's or publisher's prior consent in any form of binding or
cover other than that in which it is published and
without a similar condition including this condition being imposed
on the subsequent purchaser.

A CIP record for this book
is available from the British Library

ISBN 978-1-907211-86-7

Preface

The significance of the corporation bus went beyond its primary purpose, which was taking people to and from work, school, college, church, football and rugby matches, shopping, dance halls, pubs and cinemas.

Just as importantly, the corporation bus was an icon that, just over 40 years ago, uniquely characterised each one of nearly 100 cities and towns in the United Kingdom, through highly distinctive liveries and local fleet branding, the centrepiece of which was the coat of arms.

Corporation buses were a great source of local pride, even among citizens not normally disposed to the municipal ethos; people really did refer to them as "*our* buses", something considered unthinkable today. Moreover, their replacement, mostly by national private conglomerates, can be seen as a major milestone in the process of the cloning of Britain's High Streets: first it was buses, then it became shops.

The corporation bus, therefore, is a metaphor not only for a lost era, but also for the lost individuality of so many of the cities and large towns of Great Britain.

Front page illustrations

Main: A Walsall Corporation trolleybus about to pick up off-peak passengers in the early 1960's. *Omnicolour*

Inset: Southport Corporation enjoyed a reputation for maintaining the bodywork of its buses in pristine condition. *Omnicolour*

Top: Every corporation bus carried the coat of arms of the municipality. This is Edinburgh. *Author*

Rear cover illustrations, all Omnicolour

List of Contents

Municipal bus operators – 1960	vii
Introduction	ix

Chapters

1.	Southern England – A coastal string of pearls	1
2.	West Midlands – Black Country, blue buses	25
3.	Lancashire South-West and Cheshire – Both sides of the Mersey	38
4.	Lancashire South-East – Centre of the universe	56
5.	Lancashire North – Barrow, Blackpool and beyond	74
6.	North-East England – Tyne to Tees	90
7.	Yorkshire and Lincolnshire – Bus Ridings	102
8.	East Midlands and East Anglia – Nottingham lace and Norfolk Broads	132
9.	Wales – Small is beautiful	147
10.	Scotland, N. Ireland, Isle of Man – Over the border and across the sea	159
11.	Managers and Men – The brains and the brawn	175
12.	Oozing Civic Pride – Branding and livery	187
13.	All Wired Up – The trolleybus towns	194
14.	Missing Municipals – Buses were not their thing	201
15.	1969-74 – The giants come tumbling down	207
16.	Beyond 1986 – Picked off, one by one	214
17.	Preserved for Posterity – Where to catch a vintage 'Corpy'	220
Bibliography		225
Index		230

Municipal Bus Operators – 1960

Aberdare, Aberdeen, Accrington, Ashton-under-Lyne

Barrow-in-Furness, Bedwas & Machen, Belfast, Birkenhead, Birmingham, Blackburn, Blackpool, Bolton, Bournemouth, Bradford, Brighton, Burnley (Colne and Nelson), Burton on Trent, Bury

Caerphilly, Cardiff, Chester, Chesterfield, Colchester, Colwyn Bay, Coventry

Darlington, Darwen, Derby, Doncaster, Douglas, Dundee

Eastbourne, Edinburgh, Exeter

Gelligaer, Glasgow, Great Yarmouth, Grimsby/Cleethorpes

Halifax, Hartlepool, Haslingden, Huddersfield,

Ipswich

Kingston upon Hull

THE CORPORATION BUS

Lancaster, Leeds, Leicester, Leigh, Lincoln, Liverpool, Llandudno, Lowestoft, Luton, Lytham St Annes

Maidstone, Manchester, Merthyr Tydfil, Middlesbrough, Morecambe & Heysham

Newcastle upon Tyne, Newport, Northampton, Nottingham

Oldham

Plymouth, Pontypridd, Portsmouth, Preston

Ramsbottom, Rawtenstall, Reading, Rochdale, Rotherham

Salford, Sheffield, Southampton, Southend-on-Sea, Southport, South Shields, St Helens, SHMD*, Stockport, Stockton on Tees, Sunderland, Swindon

Tees-side**, Todmorden

Wallasey, Walsall, Warrington, West Bridgford, West Bromwich, West Hartlepool, West Monmouthshire, Widnes, Wigan, Wolverhampton

---

*Joint board - Stalybridge, Hyde, Mossley and Dukinfield

**Joint board comprising Eston UDC and Middlesbrough Corporation but separate from the latter's main municipal undertaking

Introduction

More than a people carrier

During the 1950's and 1960's the number of ordinary British families able to afford an annual summer holiday reached unprecedented levels, even if most breaks were taken within these islands, principally in 'kiss me quick' resorts dotted around the coastline.

Those who went through the experience have often reflected on how the final morning of their holiday was one of deep depression and sadness; some have even compared the atmosphere as something akin to a death in the family. For the soon to be ex-holidaymakers realised that another 50 weeks of hard graft lay ahead before they returned to the same small hotel or boarding house in the same resort the following year (as many people did in those days). Few, if any, could look forward to autumn or spring breaks in the Canaries sunshine back then.

Because of this the journey back to reality began with everyone in a neo-funereal mood, and not until the halfway stage did spirits begin to lift somewhat, something that increased with the gradual appearance of familiar sights as the train or coach neared the place its passengers called home.

THE CORPORATION BUS

However, for many home-comers the most familiar, and reassuring, sight of all was – of all things - a bus. Not just any old bus, mind you, but a *corporation* bus; one that was branded with the name of their particular town or city, bore a unique livery, wore the municipal coat of arms on the side panels and sported a well-known local landmark on its front destination screen.

As has been said by holiday returnees thousands of times with reference to almost a hundred different locations: "The first glimpse of a corporation bus was a signal that you were nearly home."

These days any holidaymaker, whether returning from Scarborough or the Seychelles, would be hard put to make a connection between a bus and the place they call home, because around 90 per cent of the municipal operators who existed in the 1960's have been replaced by national conglomerates, most of whom put corporate branding before local identity. With the great majority of urban bus fleets now in the hands of a few national operators, so many of them all seem to look much the same and in some cases *are* the same. For example, there is now absolutely no difference in colour and branding between the leading provider of city buses in Aberdeen, Leeds and Portsmouth.

One of the complaints about contemporary Britain is the way our town centres have been cloned by the consolidation of nationally- and internationally-owned retailers so that one High Street does not look much different from another. In retrospect this cloning began not with shops but with the loss of local identity on buses.

It is this sense of something worthwhile having been lost that motivated the decision to write *The Corporation Bus*. In some respects the book is more about changing

INTRODUCTION

social mores than about buses; there is little, if any, reference to manufacturers' bodies, engine horse power or registration numbers, aspects which so appeal to the bus enthusiast, although I would like to think at least some of their number will still find in this something of interest.

Rather, this book is about the connection between the corporation bus and the communities it served – which for the most part it did admirably. There is, in the opinion of the author, a direct correlation between the demise of the corporation bus and positive aspects of our earlier lives that have fallen by the wayside in the (otherwise welcome) march of material progress; aspects such as civic pride, community, a sense of shared responsibility.

The following is an example. When boarding a corporation bus late on a Friday or Saturday evening, it was not uncommon to find a uniformed police officer seated near the rear platform. This was not in anticipation of any trouble; he was simply either on his way to the police station to start his shift or returning home having just completed a shift. Yet his very presence was wonderfully reassuring for passengers and crew alike. Nowadays, the only time one is likely to encounter uniformed police on a bus is *after* a criminal offence or other anti-social act has taken place.

As the sun began to set on the golden age of the late 1950's, the next decade ushered in harder times, brought about by rising costs and changing social habits. Yet the corporation bus proved resilient and until the very end of the 1960's only one of the undertakings that had been in operation at the end of world war two, had thrown in the towel following a rather silly trade union dispute, while two other minnows sensibly merged. The real hammer blow came in the very last months of 1969, with the implementation of the Transport Act, passed by parliament a year earlier. Between 1 October 1969 and 1 January, 1970, and against the wishes of most municipal operators, four new passenger transport executives took over the assets and staff of 19 municipal fleets, including the three largest in England, i.e. Birmingham, Manchester and Liverpool. By April 1974, further PTE growth had spelled the end of the corporation bus in eight more cities and towns, while simultaneous local government reorganisation meant the very word 'corporation' was dropped from the fleetnames of those undertakings that remained. Deregulation in 1986 saw the survivors under assault again - not from regional government this time but from rival private operators.

Although parts of the content take us from the earliest municipal bus services at the beginning of the 20th century, to 1974, and in some cases beyond, the book uses as its benchmark the dawn of the 1960's, when the sun was setting on a long Indian summer for the corporation bus.

Still, I trust the image provided in these chapters is not too sepia tinted. Some undertakings were better run than others and the public were, on occasions, prone to complain about the corporation bus, as they do about any other public service – e.g. drivers ignoring requests to stop, conductors giving up 'cheek', overcrowding, rowdy fellow passengers, poor timekeeping, etc. And during what was for many undertakings, the last decade, standards undoubtedly fell at a time of virtually full employment, when management vainly competed for staff with other industries that offered not only better pay but also superior working patterns.

INTRODUCTION

But for all that there was a strong symbiosis between corporation buses and the locals whom they served and who, as ratepayers, were ostensibly shareholders in the enterprise. People really did refer to a corporation bus as one of "*ours*", a statement that would be unthinkable among passengers travelling by bus today.

It is this connection that *The Corporation Bus* seeks to celebrate – and to mark for posterity the virtual passing of an icon in which every member of the community had a share, and not just as fare-paying passengers.

1

Southern England

A coastal string of pearls

In its heyday, the corporation bus could be found as far north as Aberdeen and as far south as Plymouth but, in retrospect, it seems to have been most at home somewhere in the geographical middle, specifically the industrial and commercial heartlands of Lancashire and the West Riding of Yorkshire.

It is somewhat ironic, therefore, that the story began not in Manchester, Leeds or any of their densely populated satellites but in a sedate, conservative holiday resort on the coast of rural Sussex.

With a growing population and rising visitor levels, early in the 20th century councillors in **Eastbourne** turned their thoughts to providing adequate public transport within the borough. This was a time when what came to be known as 'tramway mania' had gripped cities and towns around the country but Eastbourne felt reluctant to join in because the prospect of overhead wiring and stanchion poles on the graceful streets of the coastal borough were an anathema to a large proportion of the local population.

THE CORPORATION BUS

A solution would have been to adopt (as was the case in some parts of London), the conduit system, which meant that the power source was buried beneath the roadway, obviating the need for overhead wires. But this was considered too expensive even for most large cities and for a small borough like Eastbourne the cost would have been prohibitive. As an alternative, therefore, the council decided to launch a service between Eastbourne Station and Meads, at the foot of Beachy Head, via Grand Parade, using petrol engine buses – despite their technology and comfort being inferior to that of trams. Thus, the world's first continuous corporation bus service was born on 12 April 1903

Two single-deck and two double-deck vehicles were used for the landmark event. Later, when service numbers were introduced this became the No.6 and lasted for more than 80 years, not being withdrawn in 1984.

Gradually, more services were introduced to serve the resident population and by the 1920's the backbone of a network that existed for the remainder of the century was in place.

The hub of the Eastbourne network was the area around the railway station and any many a visitor alighting there for the first time was immediately struck by the sight of the local buses, in their attractive blue and primrose livery, and bearing the legend EASTBOURNE CORPORATION with the coat of arms placed between.

Eastbourne was always a small network and service numbers were introduced only gradually, and it would appear somewhat reluctantly, from the 1940's. Initially, some services would show two different numbers – one for the outward and another for the return journey – something that sometimes caused confusion even among locals who used the buses regularly. However, he system was simplified by the 1960's, settling down to a simple, 15-route service chart. There were a series of stances just outside the railway station and this was officially described as the corporation's own "bus station".

One feature of the Eastbourne undertaking was the number of open-toppers used for seafront services during the holiday season. Initially these were standard double-deck vehicles with their roofs removed but by the 1960's purpose-built open-toppers were in use. In the early 1960's the 56-strong fleet contained just two single-deckers.

Variations of the same colour scheme were used. The initial and most well-known was the blue / primrose livery, with open top seafront buses painted white. This was progressively replaced from around 1968 by cream with light blue lining, but this was again superseded by a deeper cream (known as 'vellum') and a darker blue from 1974 onwards, apparently due to the difficulty in obtaining specific shades in relatively small quantities.

Eastbourne Buses, as the operation became known, survived for more than 20 years after bus deregulation in 1986 but in the spring of 2009 – despite earlier having taken on a French private sector partner as a minority shareholder – the world's oldest continuous municipal bus operator was sold to Stagecoach.

The other municipal transport undertaking in Sussex, **Brighton** did not appear to share Eastbourne's qualms about tramway overhead structure, despite the many examples of Georgian architecture in the town centre and seafront. A relatively large tram system was built up and, indeed, remained intact until 1939, when closure came about over a matter of months.

That year was also significant in transport terms as it saw the introduction of a joint co-ordination agreement between Brighton Corporation and the Brighton, Hove & District Omnibus Company, by then a wholly owned subsidiary of Thomas Tilling Ltd.

The agreement provided for the pooling of receipts and running expenses in the ratio of 72.5 per cent to BH&D and 27.5 per cent to the corporation. A joint operating area came into force covering Brighton, Hove, Portslade, Rottingdean and Southwick, with each concern responsible for the purchase and maintenance of their own vehicles and buildings. Both concerns operated trolleybuses and the agreement gave the corporation sole responsibility for the fixed equipment and the company the right to run 20 per cent of the mileage. Much later, in 1961, with growing urbanisation, the area agreement would be extended to include Southdown Motor Services.

The future of the corporation trolleybuses seemed secure in 1951 when overhead was erected to enable them to service the giant Hollingbury housing estate, on the edge of the Sussex Downs, which had grown up after the end of world war two. However within five years the corporation decided to abandon trolleybuses, even though these swift, silent vehicles were in their element on the steep gradient to Hollingbury and other hilly destinations. An official timetable for closure was not set at the time but nevertheless was achieved by 1961.

The hub of the system was the Old Steine, whose giant oval shape provided an ideal turning circle in trolleybus days and the overhead wires – three abreast at some points – contrasted starkly with the Georgian architecture, especially the iconic Brighton Pavilion, with it historic association with George lV.

Brighton Corporation livery (and that of the company) was for many years a deep red with cream relief. Since the 1938 agreement all corporation and company buses had carried the fleetname Brighton, Hove & District Transport, supplemented, in the case of corporation owned buses, by the coat of arms of Brighton. Following the 1961 agreement, corporation buses displayed 'Brighton Corporation Transport' on their lower side panels while the company vehicles showed simply Brighton, Hove & District. In 1970 the livery on corporation buses became blue and white.

Brighton Borough Transport superseded the corporation name with local government reorganisation in 1974, although 'Corporation" could still be seen on buses for several years afterwards. As was the case elsewhere, the department became a company in 1986 but remained in local authority ownership until 1993 when it was sold to its employees, who traded under Brighton Blue Bus.

The current owner is the Go-Ahead Group, which as Go Ahead Northern had previously purchased Brighton Hove & District. Go Ahead quickly moved to integrate the Brighton Blue Bus and BHD fleets, re-branded the new joint operation 'Brighton & Hove' and returned to the colour scheme associated with the joint service regime during corporation days – probably the only occasion that a former municipal fleet was taken over by one of the 'nationals' and ended up looking more like the 'original' than previously.

In transport terms, **Southampton** is better known for majestic ocean-going liners than buses but it has a claim to fame regarding the latter too.

THE CORPORATION BUS

In July 1901, almost two years ahead of Eastbourne, Southampton Corporation launched the world's first municipal bus service, which operated between the Clock Tower and Northam. However, the Southampton service was withdrawn permanently in December of that year following complaints of unreliability and the continuity of the Eastbourne service has seen it recognised as the true 'first'.

Difficulty with pioneering buses was not the only problem affecting Southampton Corporation at the turn of the last century. Between 1898, when the council took over operation of the company-run tramway system, until 1923, the undertaking had no less than six managers.

Things changed with the appointment, in 1923, of Percival Baker, which was the start of a reign under the one manager for more than 30 years, during which time the tramway was further extended, then abandoned and the modern bus fleet and service network created.

Paradoxically, given the high turnover of earlier managers, Mr Baker's successor, Gilbert Armstrong, was also a long stayer, holding the post for almost the next 20 years following the retirement of the former.

Corporation motorbus services began in earnest when, in 1919, six Thorneycroft single-deck vehicles were purchased. Double-deckers were initially six-axle but in 1930 two-axle versions arrived and these became the norm. By the outbreak of world war two, just under 30 bus services were being operated by the corporation.

Initial service numbers were from 1 to 10 (although for some unknown reason numbers did not apply to single-deckers) and from 1948 tram replacement services began at No. 11.

Southampton Corporation closed the last of its tram routes in December 1949, by which time it had become the last municipal operator of tramways in the south of England.

In addition to extending bus routes, Mr Baker also embarked on a programme of vehicle renewal and by the mid-1950's all the pre-war vehicles had been replaced. Route expansion continued and the bus network penetrated new housing estates (such as Millbrook, Harefield and Thornhill) that were built in the 1950's. A joint services agreement with the Hants and Dorset bus company, covering the outer suburbs, was also established.

However a fully integrated service network did not emerge until 1977 when the Itchen Bridge (which replaced a 'floating bridge' or ferry) opened and joined up the west and expanding eastern part of the city. Only then did the route pattern completely end its association with the original tram services.

But for a brief experiment with blue and ivory during the 1920's, livery for both trams and buses was always red with white relief but towards the end of the life of the undertaking, the colours were gradually reversed

When city status was achieved in 1964, the fleet name was changed from Southampton Corporation Transport to City of Southampton Transport – which, on deregulation in 1986 was altered again, this time to the simpler, but less distinguished, Southampton CityBus – with the coat of arms removed, of course.

The six municipal undertakings along the English south coast have been described as 'a string of pearls'. If so, then the next stone we come to is **Portsmouth**, which opened the 20th century by taking official ownership of the local privately operated horse tramway company on 1 January 1901.

The corporation trams dominated the streets for the next 18 years as Portsmouth did not introduce motorbuses until 1919, the initial models being the open-top double-deckers, and as the fleet grew the tram network withered, being finally abandoned in 1936.

After 1945, peace broke out in more ways than one for the naval city. In July 1946 the corporation and Southdown Motor Services entered into an agreement over joint running on various services, allowing both operators to pool mileage and receipts in a proportion of 57 per cent to the former and 43 to the latter.

The first corporation trolleybuses had entered service in 1934 and the system was gradually extended until Portsmouth became a medium-sized operator of the trackless electric vehicles. Trolleybuses initially carried letters to identify services but this were gradually integrated with the numbers carried by the motorbuses.

The first sign of trolleybus retraction came in 1951 when the Copnor to Floating Bridge route was replaced by motorbuses but this was more than compensated for by the erection of new overhead between Milton, Copnor and Hilsea. This resulted in a number of service extensions by trolleybus and for a short while this mode of transport seemed secure.

Although the transport manager had recommended abandonment of the trolleybuses in favour of motorbuses because of the substantial expenditure required to modernise vehicles and infrastructure, it was not until 1958 that the council approved his recommendations and the gradual abandonment of the trolleybus system began. At this time trolleybuses made up around a quarter of a *circa* 200-strong fleet.

On 27 July 1963, the final day of trolleybus operation was marked without ceremony, as the last vehicle (No. 313, a 1951 BUT 9611T), completed the final journey on the Dockyard-South Parade Pier-Eastney-Copnor-Cosham route.

In 1958 one-man operation was introduced when several older vehicles had their folding doors converted to lever operation. They were used initially to replace some of the less well-loaded journeys between Hilsea and Paulsgrove, which was primarily a double-deck operated route. Dual-door single-deck vehicles made their appearance in 1960, again for one-man operation, but with facilities for standee passengers, increasing their capacity.

As a non-metropolitan district council, Portsmouth retained its municipal fleet after reorganisation of local government in 1974 but it did not survive deregulation in 1986 for long, ignominiously selling out to – of all people – a consortium representing Southampton CityBus, although what remains of the once-proud Portsmouth undertaking has had several owners since then.

The form of perambulation most associated with **Bournemouth** is the bath chair rather than the bus but although popular with the elderly, the town has never been the coastal retirement home of legend.

In reality, Bournemouth has always been a diverse and thriving place that appealed to visitors of all ages, attracted by seven miles of beach, a wide choice of shopping, extensive night-time entertainment, and all of it set within a "garden city" by the sea.

THE CORPORATION BUS

Even out of season, by the early 1960's Bournemouth boasted a relatively large resident population of *circa* 150,000, whose local transport requirements were met by one of the most efficient municipal undertakings boasting one of the most attractive fleets in the land.

Bournemouth Corporation operated an open-sided bus service during the summer months as early as 1906 but it was not until the late 1920's that motorbuses began to emerge in any great numbers. Express services between extremes of the town were introduced and when Bournemouth's boundary began to be extended north-west into parts of Dorset, local services previously operated by the Hants & Dorset motorbus company were given over to the corporation.

At the time Bournemouth operated a 'main line' tramway extending from Christchurch in the east all the way to Poole in the west, complemented by a north south 'side line' terminating in the town centre.

However, impressed by the trolleybus system being built up in Wolverhampton, the corporation decided on this form of transport as a replacement for the trams, the last of which ran in 1936. The initial trolleybus lines more or less replicated those of the trams, although in the west this was truncated at the borough boundary – Poole having decided to choose Hants & Dorset to service the transport needs of the town.

For the remainder of the 1930's – and even during world war two – the trolleybus network continued to expand and eventually extended to 29 route miles. One interesting feature was the Christchurch terminus, where the bus was parked on a turntable and, with a hefty 'heave' from the driver and conductor, was turned round to face the way it came.

Overhead wires reached Bournemouth Pier in 1950 and a year later an additional link was made to the depot at Mallard Road but expansion then came to an abrupt halt and the next dozen years was a period of consolidation. In early 1963 the council decided, in principle, not to order any new trolleybuses. Although actual closures were low key at first, the complete north-south 'side' routes to Moordown, Winton, Charminster and Wallisdown were dewired between 1965 and 1966, leaving just the main line "eastern routes" to Boscombe, Tuckton and Christchurch. These were closed in April 1969, with some of the buses operating them just seven years old.

Bournemouth owned more trolleybuses than motorbuses at the start of the 1960's and it was only with the 1965 closures that the latter became the dominant form of transport

In 1974, when Bournemouth lost is corporation status, the fleet name was changed to Bournemouth Transport and the maroon/chocolate that had provided relief to the main colour of primrose (yellow) was replaced by blue.

The manager at the time, Ian Cunningham, was a keen advocate of PR and when, in 1982, a marketing exercise among local people concluded that his buses were colloquially referred to as "the yellows", the trading name was changed to 'Yellow Buses, Bournemouth' and so it remained for more than a quarter of a century until the company was taken over by Transdev in 2008.

The most southerly and westerly point on the British mainland where one could travel by corporation bus was that other great naval city, **Plymouth**.

The first of these municipal vehicles – all single-deck - entered service in 1921 to cover areas not served by the

THE CORPORATION BUS

tramway network. They were painted in the then tramway livery of yellow and, with typical West Country understatement, had the title PLYMOUTH CORPORATION BUSES in large script placed on the side panels. However, due to their rather fragile bodywork and the condition of the roads, they were not popular with passengers, who called them "boneshakers" and the future of the tramway network seemed assured.

In 1929 a new manager, C J Jackson, was appointed. He had come from Oldham and quickly made a decision to replace the yellow livery with the maroon and cream associated with his previous undertaking in Lancashire. At that time rapid advances in motorbus design and construction were being made and quickly into his tenure of office, Mr Jackson recommended complete replacement of the trams by buses. This was carried out efficiently, so that by the outbreak of world war two only a single tram route remained although, miraculously, that survived until peace returned nearly six years later.

Plymouth, being a key naval base, suffered terribly from German bombing during the early part of the war, particularly in March 1941 when the old city centre was virtually destroyed. However, life had to go on and after many years of wrangling, Plymouth Corporation and the Western National bus company put together a joint services agreement. This led to Western National serving inner urban areas and also to the somewhat unusual site of a corporation bus skirting the edge of Dartmoor or terminating at a picture-postcard English country village (complete with thatched cottages and village green) such as Meavey.

The agreement divided the revenue, mileage and operating expenses on the basis of 80 per cent to the corporation and 20 per cent to the company. The joint committee would settle the matters of fares, timetables and alterations to services although they would not have jurisdiction over services that ran partly in and partly out of the agreed area and which had a minimum single fare of two shillings and sixpence. Interestingly, traffic inspectors could board and carry out their inspections on the vehicles of either party.

The agreement was formally approved by the full council in April 1942 and became operative from that October.

With the end of hostilities, work began on rebuilding the city centre and the impressive dual carriageway, Royal Parade, became the focal point for cross-city bus services. Among the new buildings on Royal Parade was the Theatre Royal – a replacement for an earlier theatre of the same name, which had not been destroyed by German bombs but demolished in 1938 to make way for a cinema. Unfortunately, buses terminating here began to carry the somewhat bland 'City centre' on their destination screens rather than the more romantic 'Theatre', which had been the designated destination for trams and pre-war buses.

Peace also brought about massive developments of housing on the periphery of the city at various locations, include g Efford, Ham and Kings Tamerton. This brought about the extensions of routes 9 and 16 and several new services – 17, 28, 32, 33, 34, 35, 84, 84A and 84B. In 1950 Plymouth absorbed adjoining rural areas from which grew the massive Southway Estate and a new service, No 40, was launched to serve it.

Towards the end of the 1950's the joint services committee agreed to renumber the services, which up to

THE CORPORATION BUS

then had operated under a 'series' system; the 80 and 90 series were abolished and numbers were rearranged to run from 1 to 57 which, apart from being simpler, enabled the removal of many of the awkward A and B suffixes.

Sadly, although almost inevitably, the agreement did not survive deregulation after 1986 and at the time of writing Plymouth Citybus had just been sold to the Go-Ahead group – despite a strong campaign against by the busmens' trade union.

In the summer of 1975, while enjoying the sea air in Torquay, I was delighted to come across a passenger-carrying bus, resplendent in the full livery of **Exeter** Corporation Transport, even though the undertaking had been sold to Devon General four years previously. I remember also shaking my head in amazement that a local authority could have dispensed with such a handsome civic brand (the green paintwork was in beautiful condition and the coat of arms and legend 'Exeter' were prominent on the two lower side panels), in the way that one feels bewilderment when a friend or colleague dumps a good-looking female partner for a plainer alternative.

Unbeknown to me at the time, Exeter Corporation had actually tried to dispose of its municipal transport undertaking at least three times, finally being successful in 1971. The first negotiations were as far back as 1921, when trams reigned supreme but Devon General (which at the time had been in existence for only two years) felt unable to take on the commitment.

The trams closed in 1931 and the replacement corporation buses used route letters (A to H), rather than numbers, mainly to distinguish them from the numbered Devon General buses operating in the locality.

With services returning to normal after world war two, the corporation and Devon General began talks about a joint services agreement and this was signed in January 1947, the area involved taking in a ten-mile radius of the city centre. This gave Devon General increased access to city passengers but the *quid pro quo* was that corporation buses could now be seen in the unlikely setting of picture postcard Devon villages in the same manner as Plymouth.

In 1948 new routes, including K (to Pennsylvania); CW (to Countess Wear), and J (to Crossmead), were introduced. This situation lasted for the next 20 years when there was a major change of services and timetables in 1968 with the corporation operating 15 services, numbered from A to U (but with various gaps).

Despite the money saved by the agreement, in 1954 the council again approached Devon General (much bigger by now) about selling the undertaking but although a deal was agreed in principle, it broke down over safeguards of the jobs and pension rights of corporation staff.

Exeter Corporation decided to make another go of the undertaking and appointed a new manager, William Austin, with a brief of turning things round. By all accounts he did a good job but was unable to stem the effects of rising car ownership and alternative entertainment outlets which did not require locals to use buses as frequently as before. Therefore negotiations resumed with Devon General and on 31 March 1970 the last corporation service bus – a return journey from Crediton to Exeter – entered the depot.

Happily, some vehicles remained in municipal livery until as late as 1977 – hence my opportunity to view a

THE CORPORATION BUS

'working' Exeter Corporation bus, even though the organisation had already passed into history.

Moving back east, **Swindon** is something of a paradox – located in overwhelmingly rural Wiltshire but at the same time a town with a great industrial heritage, especially in respect of the massive Great Western railway works, which once dominated the local employment scene.

Therefore, despite this being the West Country, Swindon in some respects took on the appearance of a Lancashire mill town and the corporation bus seemed very much at home here as a result. The first of these put in an appearance in 1927, services were expanded a year later and accelerated between May and July 1929 when the last of the town's tram routes – which had been launched in 1904 - were abandoned. The advantage of the bus for a smallish undertaking was shown by the fact that by the 1930's the corporation was operating nine bus services whereas there had been only three tram services covering less than four miles in total.

Further expansion of the network was initially curtailed by wartime restrictions but Swindon then became part of the 'war economy' and new corporation bus services were introduced to take workers to and from new factories that began to spring up on the outskirts of town.

In the 1950s further expansion was required to serve new housing and Penhill, Walcot East, Lawn, Park North and Park South. After 1960 further additional services were introduced to serve the Princess Margaret Hospital, Covingham and Greenmeadow. At the time the undertaking was operating around 70 buses.

Tram, and initially bus, livery was maroon and cream but in the late 1930's this was changed to dark blue with a cream relief and remained throughout the life of the undertaking.

The first one-man operated service started in 1969 and had become the norm when, in April 1974, Swindon Corporation Transport changed to Thamesdown Transport, when this became the name of the new district authority, albeit centred on Swindon.

In 2000, Thamesdown District Council gave way to Swindon Borough Council, after a longstanding campaign by local residents to have the name of their town returned to the administrative map of England. However Thamesdown Transport, despite being still in local authority control, declined to follow suit and reintroduce Swindon as the fleetname, arguing that Thamesdown better represented the present operating area – much expanded since the days of Swindon Corporation Transport.

Thanks in part to the sterling efforts of the local trolleybus preservation society, **Reading** – lying just under 40 miles west of central London – is, perhaps, the most chronicled of all the southern municipals.

In December 1919 Reading Corporation launched its first motorbus route – between the joint stations and Oxford Road. Six months later a second service, between Lower Caversham and Redlands Road, followed and this showed the great advantage of the bus because it meant that the corporation could now serve folks living on the north bank of the River Thames without the need to lay track and erect overhead on Caversham Bridge.

In a scenario mirrored across the country, the buses soon began to parallel tram services and then replace them altogether, the tramway system in Reading being brought to a close in 1939 after 36 years of operation.

Prior to world war one Reading had taken steps to initiate a trolleybus route over Caversham Bridge but the outbreak of hostilities put that on hold and by the time the conflict was over minds had changed and motor-buses preferred.

However, by the early 1930's great strides had been made in the performance (and design) of trolleybuses and in July 1936 they made their first passenger-carrying appearance in Reading, working a north-south route between Caversham Bridge and Whitley Road. This was later extended south to Whitley Wood, with a branch leaving Basingstoke Road to Northumberland Avenue but at the northern end trolleys never did get to cross Caversham Bridge.

This route was known as the 'side line', which was crossed in the centre of town by the 'main line' – a six-mile stretch of wiring between Wokingham Road in the east to Tilehurst in the west, with branches also off to Liverpool Road and Kentwood respectively. The two lines met at the junction of Broad Street and St Mary's Butts and this was the busy hub of the system. There were other town centre turning points on St Mary's Butts itself and at Reading General station.

Although the trolleybus began to fall from grace by the late 1950's, in Reading at least its future seemed safe. At the start of the 1960's Reading had more double deck trolleybuses than double deck motorbuses, new trolley-buses were being delivered up to 1961, an extension of Whitley Wood was made in 1963 and in 1964 one local councillor declared that they were "here to stay". Yet within two years this policy was put into reverse and the last Reading trolleybus ran on November 1968, despite a valiant, thought-provoking and professional campaign by the local enthusiasts' group.

Reading was a very expansionist undertaking and unlike many other southern municipals did not care to involve itself in joint agreements with the local prime 'country' operator. Thus, on the eve of local government reorganisation in 1974, a substantial number of Reading's mileage was outside the boundary, especially in the new private housing estates that were mushrooming to the east (London end) of the town.

After deregulation, Reading coped with competition from both national and local predators better than most and at the time of writing is undoubtedly one of the most successful of the remaining council-owned companies.

Latterly, the management has put much emphasis on route branding to win passengers, the prime one being the 17, Wokingham Road to Tilehurst. In earlier times this was the showcase trolleybus route so its continuing special treatment must have given those hardy local enthusiasts some consolation.

Luton was one of the lesser-known municipal undertakings, perhaps because of its relative proximity to London and the fact that Bedfordshire was not exactly fertile corporation bus territory.

Luton Corporation operated its first bus service – as a tram replacement – in February 1932 but its existence threatened to be short lived. Being within the London travel to work area, Luton looked ripe for absorption in the new London Transport Board being set up in 1933. However, although 11 southern municipal undertakings were taken over by London Transport, Luton was not one of them.

Three years earlier the corporation bought over three local private companies – the Union Jack Omnibus Company, XL Motor Services and Bluebird Services. The purchase opened up a great deal of territorial scope for new routes but Eastern National objected. The issue was solved by the formation of a 21-year agreement that not only divided up current services in Luton and district but also encouraged a joint approach to the planning and delivery of new services in the future. This arrangement was superseded by a later, simpler, agreement in 1948, which meant that services would be split 50/50 and fares pooled and divided in the same manner.

Continuing its role as a forward-looking utility, the corporation broke new ground by launching a service between the town centre and Luton Airport in 1937. Meanwhile, Luton and Eastern National settled down to two decades of peaceful coexistence, during which corporation livery changed from maroon with white relief to red and white and then, finally, to all over red, in the mode of London Transport.

However, the financial situation started to deteriorate and in 1967 the corporation began a process to replace all rear engine double-deckers with single-deckers, even though one-man operation was now permitted on both. Up to the mid-sixties, the fleet had been entirely double-decker.

Towards the end of the decade negotiations about renewing the 1948 joint services agreement with United Counties (successor to Eastern National) turned into a takeover discussion. This was concluded to the satisfaction of both parties and on 4 January 1970 Luton Corporation Transport went out of existence – the first municipal transport undertaking in the South of

England to do so since the formation of London Transport 37 years earlier.

Corporation buses made their first appearance on the streets of **Southend** in 1914, principally as tramway feeders, but the new vehicles were not well received by the public and the service closed two years later.

When buses did reappear, after an absence of ten years, it was in the form of trolleybuses. These proved to be more popular and the system was extended as the trams retracted, one line actually operating along the seafront from the famous Kursal amusement park to Thorpe Bay Corner. As in other towns, extension of the Southend trolleys stalled during world war two, but unlike most other systems, there was no great enthusiasm for further extensions after 1945 and the system was gradually run down, closing in 1954.

Meanwhile, the first corporation motorbus had reappeared by 1930 and inevitably these formed the mainstay of local municipal transport services. One problem for Southend – which seemed to be prevalent among municipal operators on the south coast – was that they faced intensive competition from entrenched company operators. Without the protection of 'monopoly area' status, the corporation had no alternative but to try and reach an agreement with the main private operator, Westcliff Motor Services, which had a much larger network than its name might imply. In 1945 agreement was reached for the establishment of a joint services area, in which the takings would be divided between the corporation, Westcliff (both 45.9 per cent) and the then minority Eastern National (8.2 per cent). However agreement could not be achieved with other excluded operators and the scheme collapsed. Some joint running was later achieved on a route-by-route basis but full co-ordination did not happen until 1955. The area covered extended to just under 100 square miles and the network was operated under 'Southend Joint Services'.

For many years Southend had operated without the need for service numbers but these were gradually introduced from 1944. To avoid duplication with Westcliff Motor Service routes, corporation services were generally numbered 50 and above – although this all changed following the co-ordination agreement. Many services terminated in the town centre – no less than 16 at Victoria Circus/Victoria Station, two more at Central Station and another at Pier Hill.

Southend operated around 90 vehicles at its peak, all wearing an appropriate livery of light (sea) blue with cream relief.

With the western part of Essex so influenced by London, it is hardly surprising that the two municipal undertakings were located in the east of the county.

The smaller of these, **Colchester**, was a superb representative of the genre, not only operating an efficient service which gave comprehensive coverage to the borough but also taking cognisance of the contribution made by municipal buses to local identify and civic pride.

Colchester Corporation began the replacement of its small tram system with buses in 1928 and all were gone by the end of 1929. In 1937 the corporation rebuffed an offer from Eastern National to purchase the town routes; having reaffirmed its independence, a change to a new livery of blue and white was toyed with but in the end it was decided to stick with the traditional Tuscan red and cream.

Colchester went into expansive mode after world war two but falling revenues caused a retrenchment in services, which by the end of the 1950's read: 1/1A, Parsons Heath to Dugard Avenue/Prettygate; 2/2A; Ipswich Road to Severalls/Mill road; 3, High Street to St Andrews Avenue; 4, Hythe to Layer Road Estate or Berechurch Camp; 5, Dugard Avenue to Bergholt Road; 5A, Lexdent to Turner Road; 6, Old Heath to Prettygate or Shrub End Estate; 7, Mersea Road or Monkwick Estate to North Station.

This also involved a reduction in frequencies but in 1961 and, in contrast to many other municipal operators, timings were increased again and more services were introduced to serve growing housing estates - Greenstead in 1961; Barnhall in 1962; St. John's in 1967 and St. Michael's in 1968. This required a 50 per cent increase in the fleet size from 40 to 60 vehicles.

Following a name change to Colchester Borough Council Transport as a result of local government reorganisation in 1974, the livery was also changed, this time to crimson and cream (after experimentation with cherry red).

Like many of the smaller undertakings, especially in the south-east of England, municipal trams in **Maidstone** were relatively short lived, lasting for just 26 years from 1904 to 1930.

The first motorbus service (on tram replacement) was inaugurated in 1929 but trolleybuses had put in an appearance a year earlier and the electric vehicles became a distinct feature of Maidstone transport for nearly 40 years. Indeed, the last trolleybus extension – to Park Wood on the Sutton Road route – took place as late as 1963, just four years before the demise of the system. At the time the fleet contained almost as many trolleybuses as motorbuses.

THE CORPORATION BUS

Trolleybuses operated a winding T-system from Barming in the north through the town centre to the Wheatsheaf junction where the wires diverted along Sutton Road and along Kent Road. Wiring was quite extensive in the town centre, allowing a number of permutations of both cross-town routes and short workings. The fume-free nature of the trolleybus was an obvious advantage in some of the narrow, quite cavernous central streets.

What made Maidstone Corporation buses (both trolley and motorbus) stand out was their very dignified ochre (light brown) colour scheme, which was unique in corporation bus circles. This livery was maintained for trolleybuses until their final abandonment but by this time a somewhat insipid light blue and white had become standard livery for motorbuses.

Service numbers (or letters) were thought unnecessary for such a small undertaking but, more surprisingly, Maidstone remained a dedicated operator of double-deck vehicles, a policy that continued right up to 1974 when Maidstone Corporation Transport became the somewhat bland Maidstone Borough Council Transport. The change also coincided with a decision to replace the double-deckers with single-deckers.

One fascinating feature of the network was the number of full and part services that terminated at public houses – indeed on a *pro rata* basis, Maidstone probably had more pubs on its bus destination screens than any other city or town in the country!

2

West Midlands

Black Country, blue buses

At some point between the two world wars the population of Glasgow was overtaken by Birmingham and the mantle of 'second city of the United Kingdom' passed from the former to the latter. Within the same period the second city emerged as the country's largest municipal bus operator.

As befits a place where many citizens earned their living through the motor car industry, Birmingham was the earliest of the big municipal operators to go 'all motorbus', although it did at one time also boast one of the largest tram systems in the country and was an early experimenter with trolleybuses.

The first corporation bus service – from Selly Oak to Rednal – was launched in 1913. The corporation must have anticipated rapid expansion of bus services because just a year later, it entered into a joint agreement – or perhaps a 'joint truce' might be a more appropriate expression – with Midland Red, whereby the former agreed not to operate beyond the city boundary while the latter agreed not to compete for fares within the city limits. Agreement or 'truce', it worked remarkably well and lasted for more than 40 years.

An experimental trolleybus service was inaugurated to Nechells in 1922 but it was not until 12 years later that a conventional service was started, along Coventry Road. However, Birmingham – unlike neighbouring Wolverhampton and Walsall – was lukewarm towards the trolleybus; only two more services were ever introduced and the 'system', if it could be called that, closed in 1952 – a year before the last tram.

Like most transport undertakings, Birmingham City Transport (the official title) emerged from world war two somewhat battered and bruised but in a remarkable programme of renewal between 1947 and 1954, purchased over 1,700 new buses to replace its entire fleet of trams, trolleybuses, along with most of the pre-war motorbuses.

The basic livery was a sombre (but very dignified) dark blue – officially 'monastrol' – lower decking with cream upper decks (sometimes with blue reliefs). The replacement buses referred to above were either Crossleys, Daimlers or Guys made to the same basic design – which was called the 'new look'. This produced a very distinctive 'Birmingham bus' that reigned in the city until the large-scale advent of rear-engine vehicles towards the end of the undertaking's life. Strangely, these vehicles had a recessed driver's window (developed, incidentally, by a manger of Midland Red) which gave them a somewhat 1930's look yet somehow added to their appeal.

Buses had replaced trams as the main form of municipal transport in the city by 1935 and by the outbreak of world war two Birmingham had the largest and most modern municipal motorbus fleet in the country.

Two events called for further expansion shortly after the end of hostilities – the start of all-night services in 1946 and the resumption of the tramway abandonment programme (after a nine-year break) in 1947. By the undertaking's heyday in the 1950's, the undertaking was operating more than 90 daytime services.

Although there were cross-city routes, a significant number of services terminated at various on-street stops and shelters in the city centre, for example at the three rail termini (New Street, Snow Hill and Moor Street) and around the main shopping area of New Street, Colmore Row and Corporation Street. However, there was no grand central area terminal, as there was in Manchester and Liverpool. One peculiarity of the network was that all services operating arterial routes contained the outer terminal on the destination board – even when the bus was city-bound.

Birmingham had two particularly interesting and well-known services, the No 8 Inner Circle and the No 11 Outer Circle – so interesting in fact that separate books were published about both and sold on the open market.

The city, like the undertaking, continued to grow and the agreement with Midland Red was renegotiated so that the corporation took over three suburban services formerly operated by the latter - Beeches Estate (new service number 52), 'Scott Arms' (51) and New Oscott (42) were taken over by the Corporation in September 1957, May 1958 and September 1958 respectively.

However, social issues, not related wholly to bus operation, began to adversely affect the department. In 1954, BCT was expelled from the Federation of Municipal Transport Employers for raising wages to try and compete for staff with Birmingham's then booming manufacturing base. Despite the additional money, BCT could not offer exemption from shift and weekend work and the policy was only partly successful.

Another socially related issue was a ban, introduced in 1962, on employees wearing turbans, which was abolished after Sikh workers went on strike.

Growing traffic congestion was also a problem, made worse in Birmingham by construction of the inner ring road and redevelopment of large parts of the city centre. However, quite apart from the obvious inconvenience that came with such a project, there was a feeling in some quarters that the road improvements being implemented by Birmingham Corporation were very much for the benefit of the private car rather than its own motorbuses.

By the early 1960's, Birmingham boasted a fleet of over 1,700 buses, the vast majority of them double-deckers, by far the largest of any public or private undertaking in the country after London Transport.

On 1 October 1969 Birmingham City Transport, along with the municipal undertakings of Wolverhampton, Walsall and West Bromwich, became part of the new West Midlands Passenger Transport Executive. It was decided to have a region-wide colour scheme, based on Birmingham livery, albeit with a slightly lighter shade of blue. So, for people who care little about these things, there was not a lot of difference in the outward appearance of buses in Birmingham. For the believer in municipal operation and local civic pride, however, the loss of the coat of arms on the lower side panels meant the operation had lost its unique identity.

The largest of the four Staffordshire undertakings, **Wolverhampton** was unusual among municipal tramway operators in choosing a surface rather than overhead electric contact method for its tramway system, mostly for aesthetic reasons. Somewhat incongruously, the corporation then went on to string up many miles of double overhead wires to power what became one of the largest trolleybus networks in the country.

However, the first bus to operate in corporation colours was of the petrol engine variety and it ran a service, launched in 1911, between Queen Square in the town centre and the increasingly industrial Park Lane area. In 1914 two more half-hourly services were introduced, to Compton and to the Rose & Crown at Penn, both from Victoria Square.

The first trolleybus service was launched in October 1923, although the buses used actually had petrol engine chassis but with the engine and generator removed. The subsequent success of the service led to a decision to replace all the existing tram routes with this method of transport.

Motorbus services also expanded to feed the new housing estates but there was a general preference towards the trolley vehicles as figures prepared for the transport department showed they had superior running costs. Consequently, new orders made during and immediately after world war two for both trolleybuses and motorbuses were heavily biased in favour of the latter in terms of numbers.

The manager of the time, Charles Owen Silvers, was enthusiastic about trolleybuses but with his retirement, in 1949, went much of the impetus behind their continued operation locally and the purchase of new trolleybuses ceased after 1950. However, a decision to abandon was not made until 1961, when there was an almost equal number of trolleybuses and motorbuses making up the 316-strong vehicle fleet. The last service to operate under the wires – which took the long route from Wolverhampton town centre to Dudley in Worcestershire – did not end until March 1967, although local people must have recognised the end was near two years before that when trolleybuses were removed from Darlington Street, the main retail thoroughfare of Wolverhampton.

One interesting feature of Wolverhampton's motor-bus activities was the corporation's variety of rural services to outlying villages and towns, which had begun in the 1920's. Destinations included Bridgnorth, Swindon Staffs, Claverly, Pattingham, Beckbury, Tong Norton, Weston-under-Lizard, Cannock and Cheslyn Hay – and they contrasted starkly with the core of the network situated in the 'Black Country'. Indeed, the Wolverhampton rural network was so extensive, that the department had to purchase a motorcycle and sidecar outfit for the inspector to be able to cope.

Wolverhampton livery was an apple green with canary yellow relief between the upper and lower deck, which provided a pleasant variation but was much reduced in size towards the end for the usual reasons of cost. Thus, of the four cities and towns whose undertakings were taken over by West Midlands Passenger Transport Executive, Wolverhampton underwent the greatest outward transformation because the PTE adopted blue for its corporate livery, a colour which – in various shades - was already in use by the other three constituent undertakings of Birmingham, Walsall and West Bromwich.

Walsall was another prolific trolleybus operator the difference being that it continued to extend its wires for some time after Wolverhampton had made the decision to abandon its system.

Corporation trams began running in 1904 and the first motorbus put in an appearance 11 years later, on an out of town route to Hednesford via Cannock. This was the first of a network of motorbus services that took Walsall colours into many of the surrounding towns and villages – indeed as far as Stafford, almost 20 miles way. Trolleybuses made an appearance in 1931 and two years later replaced to last two tram services – to Bloxwich and the joint service with Wolverhampton.

Another major development in the 1930's was the construction of a bus terminal at St Paul's Street, which served as a purpose-built town centre terminal for many years. It also included the corporation transport offices, which provided the general manager with a bird's eye view of traffic operations without having to leave his desk.

Trolleybuses usually comprised only one-fifth of the total fleet but because of the 'metropolitan' nature of the Walsall network, their presence within the borough boundary was much greater than their numbers might suggest. This was especially true from 1952 with the arrival of what turned out to be the last general manager, R Edgely Cox. An exponent of the electric vehicle, he secured legislation for a ten-year programme of expansion that permitted expansion of the wires without the time and expense of applying for parliamentary powers for each route.

Thus from 1955 he revised trolleybus services by extending the wires to new housing areas and also linking up existing wires within the town to create circular route permutations. All five 'Walsall' services – the 15, 30, 31, 32 and 33 terminated at St Paul's Street but the joint service with Wolverhampton – the 29 – stopped some distance away at Townend Street. The last extension came about in 1963 when wires were erected along Bloxwich Lane to provide a new service to Cavendish Road.

Difficulties caused by engineering construction work on the M6 motorway caused the closure of the Wolverhampton service but the basic town service survived and as late as 1969 – the final year of Walsall Corporation Transport – the manager was seeking parliamentary powers for an additional five miles of wiring. This never came to fruition, of course, but trolleybuses continued to operate in Walsall for a year after the undertaking was taken over by the West Midlands PTE.

Something of an innovator, Mr Cox helped design a trolleybus which accommodated 62 seated passengers while 15 more could queue to buy tickets (from a seated conductor) as the bus moved off. He also persuaded the Ministry of Transport to allow operation of 30ft long trolleybuses on the lighter, and less costly, two-axles.

On the motorbus front he jumped at the chance to show a, 36ft-long, 86-seater Daimler in Walsall colours at the 1968 Commercial Motor Show.

Walsall livery was unusual in using the one overall colour, in this case medium blue, albeit with yellow lining. It took a bit of getting used to but after a while looked rather impressive – especially in the futuristic Sunbeam F4A trolleybuses, with their curved fronts, and on whose design Mr Cox had a hand.

Just as West Bromwich Albion has always punched above its weight in football for a town of its size, so too did **West Bromwich** Corporation in the heyday of municipal transport.

This is all the more surprising given that West Bromwich was a relative latecomer to the municipal scene, having never operated trams (which in the town were the preserve of the South Staffordshire Tramways Company, a subsidiary of BET).

The corporation began operating motorbuses – between Dartmouth Square in the town centre and Greets Green - in 1914 and up to 1930 the fleet consisted of single-deckers after which, as was the pattern with other municipal operators, double-deckers gradually took over. Birmingham Corporation had taken over operation of the tramway to West Bromwich in 1924 but in 1939 the trams were scrapped and replaced by a bus service operated jointly by the West Bromwich and Birmingham municipalities. This and the need to serve new housing estates being built on the outskirts of the town led to a major expansion of the corporation transport department.

Service numbers were introduced in 1931 and for a time they were listed chronologically from 1 to 24. However, high numbers came into being when it was decided to retain the Birmingham tram service identification for the replacing buses –74 for Birmingham Snow Hill to Dudley Station and 75 to Wednesbury – plus 73, 76, 77, 78 and 79 for various short workings.

Several existing services were extended and new ones introduced to cater for even more housing during the 1950's and 60's. Borough services were in addition to joint ones not just with Birmingham but also with Walsall and Wolverhampton corporations and with Midland Red. Fully one third of the West Bromwich mileage was outside the borough boundary and its buses penetrated no less than 11 neighbouring local authorities.

West Bromwich had a reputation for charging some of the lowest fares in the country yet despite this the buses were well maintained and presented and the two-tone dark and light blue livery (with cream relief) was particularly attractive. And up to the very last day prior to their absorption by West Midlands PTE, the buses proudly (and defiantly?) continued to carry, in large script, the original fleet name – WEST BROMWICH CORPORATION.

The smallest of the four Staffordshire undertakings was **Burton on Trent** which in the municipal transport era was also the unofficial brewery capital of Britain, being the source of every fourth pint of beer consumed in this country at the time. The corporation introduced buses in 1924 and as in so many smaller operating towns, this soon spelled the death knell for the trams, which closed on New Year's Eve 1929. However, the first double deck buses did not put in an appearance until 1943.

By 1938 the system had grown to 12 core services and this remained in place until the mid-fifties when route extensions to Easton Road Estate and Uxbridge were made. At its height the fleet stood at 46 vehicles.

Livery had always been crimson with a little cream relief. In 1969 the Burton Civic Society wrote to the general manager requesting a chance of colour scheme "to enlighten and improve the appearance of the town" and from then on new and repainted buses were given a greater cream content.

In 1973 Midland Red submitted an offer to buy the undertaking but this was turned down. Therefore, when Burton became part of the larger East Staffordshire District Council, in April 1974 the fleet was still in municipal ownership – but the fleet name was now that of the new authority, rather than Burton upon Trent, the place with which most local bus users still identified.

Somewhat isolated geographically from Birmingham, Wolverhampton, Walsall and West Bromwich, **Coventry** Corporation Transport received a four-year plus stay of execution before being dragged into West Midlands PTE, on the launch of the new metropolitan county of the same name in 1974.

Coventry was – somewhat paradoxically, given its association with the motor industry – an early pioneer of electric trams, the first (local company) line being electrified as early as December 1895. The corporation bought over the company in 1912 and for the next 18 years greatly extended the network.

However, in 1914 the corporation also purchased six, open top, double deck motorbuses from a local firm and launched a service linking the town hall, Upper Stoke and the Fire Station. A second service – between Broadgate and Hearsall Lane – opened two months later but this and the original were abandoned in the following September when the vehicles were requisitioned by the war office.

Bus operation resumed in 1919 and the service pattern set up then provided the benchmark for the network for the rest of its existence, albeit with many extensions. Despite this being Britain's 'motor city', tramway abandonment did not begin until 1932.

The loss of vehicles was severe when Coventry was carpet bombed by the Germans on that terrible night of 14 November 1940 but just two days later the corporation had managed to establish a skeleton service using

20 vehicles and regular services were back to normal within a week.

The bombing led to a decision abandon the three remaining tram routes early the next year.

Coventry Transport shared in the post-war boom and this led to a number of new bus services and extensions. Although Coventry – thanks to the motor industry – was probably the most affluent city (in consumer terms) in the country outside the South-east, bus passenger numbers did not peak until 1955 – five to seven years after other towns and cities where there was significantly less car ownership.

After that the story in Coventry was much the same as elsewhere – declining passenger numbers, followed by fare increases to compensate for the shortfall in revenue.

The situation was not helped by staff shortages. Although this was a problem for many corporation bus operators, it was particularly acute in Coventry where jobs in the motor industry were plentiful and wages high. Therefore, the corporation eventually reached an agreement with the trade unions, which helped it compete with local private employers on wages – and (like Birmingham) was kicked out of the Federation of Municipal Transport Employers, for breaking the line.

Coventry, along with Manchester, was also a municipal pioneer of one-man operation and a programme to convert the whole undertaking was begun in August 1968. Coventry was the second largest undertaking in the West Midlands, vehicle numbers reaching around 350 at their peak.

The transport department operated a concise and simple route identification system, which by the time of the final year of operation consisted of 30 regular services. Most of these services terminated inside the city boundary, the only long distance workings of any note being the 20 and 30 to Bedworth, although corporation buses also crossed the boundary to serve the airport and the giant Chrysler plant at Ryton.

However, from 1 April 1974 this efficient, medium-sized undertaking was no more and the distinctive red livery (latterly reversed to cream with red reliefs) of the local fleet was eventually subsumed by the corporate regional blue and cream of the PTE.

Lancashire South-West and Cheshire

Both sides of the Mersey

Several prominent transport historians have described **Liverpool** as England's greatest tramway city but the corporation was also quick off the mark in acquiring its first buses, which were purchased in 1911 with the takeover of a locally-based company, Woolton Motor Omnibus Company.

The corporation purchased its first new buses in the period 1912 to 1914 and in the late 1920's showed a penchant for ordering heavy six-wheel single-deckers.

Even by the end of world war two, the bulk of Liverpool's transport service operations were still tram-based. However the manager recommended to the corporation in 1945 that because of actual and anticipated costs, the trams should be abandoned over the next 12 years. The first major closure came in 1948 when the 26/27 circular service was replaced by buses; this shaved 15 minutes off the journey time by completing it in 45 minutes instead of the 60 required by the trams. In doing so the management was able to provide a 2.5-minute frequency with 35 buses as opposed to a five-minute frequency with 30 trams. It was facts such as these – rather than some dark conspiracy between the motor industry and the oil companies, as has sometimes been alleged – that led to the general replacement of street tramways by buses in the towns and cities of Britain.

Full tramway abandonment began in earnest in 1949 and in six years, from 1952 to 1958, the size of the bus fleet rose from 769 to 1,241.

The by now familiar green livery (with cream relief) sported by Liverpool buses had been established in the mid-thirties, following the appointment, as general manager, of W.G. Marks, formerly of Nottingham. Mr Marks brought several Nottingham influences with him, including his colour preferences, and green replaced the familiar crimson that had adorned Liverpool trams and buses up to that time. By the time the 1960's arrived, pressure to cut costs had reduced the cream relief, to the detriment of the overall appearance of the buses. However the situation was improved, to some extent, by placing the legend, 'City of Liverpool' around the coat of arms.

Towards the end of the 1960's, when one man operation put in an appearance, the initial vehicles were painted in a reverse cream with green relief, as a means of distinguishing OMO buses and, presumably, helping to warn waiting members of the public to have their fares ready for boarding. However, once it became clear that OMO operation would increasingly be the norm, it was decided to retain green as the dominant colour.

Although Liverpool Corporation did operate crosstown bus routes, the majority of services began and ended in the city centre, principally at the Pier Head, which in tramway days had accommodated three giant turning circles and afterwards was the terminus for at least bus 30 services. Other city centre terminating points included Castle Street and South Castle Street, Lime Street station, Great Crosshall Street and the area around the city's impressive St George's Hall.

In 1965 a large bus station, accommodating more than 30 bays, was opened at the Pier Head although other central area terminals were retained in South Castle Street, Old Haymarket and South Thomas Street. However, by then ferry passenger traffic had passed its peak (at one time 44 per cent of Wallasey residents, on the opposite side of the Mersey, had travelled into Liverpool city centre daily to work) and this, coupled with deterioration to the fabric, led to the bus station's closure in 1991.

In the mid-1960's new services were launched to serve peripheral areas such as Tower Hill (Kirkby), Halewood and Netherley and additional works services were put on to serve the then booming local factories. However, a strike by crews in 1968 also led to the curtailment of some services and the complete abandonment of several of these.

Service numbers went from 1 to 99, with many having alphabetical suffices for short workings or other route deviations. For example, if a number was followed by a 'C', it meant the bus was routed via Church Street (the main retail thoroughfare), whereas 'D' meant via Dale Street, where Liverpool Town Hall was situated.

There were also a number of limited stop services in the '500' series and a night service using the Mersey Tunnel operated in conjunction with Birkenhead Corporation.

Liverpool's reputation as a football mad city even had a place in the corporation timetable – a full page each being devoted to the relevant bus boarding and alighting points for journeys to Anfield and Goodison Park on match days.

The bulk of services were confined to the city boundary, the exceptions being those to Prescot and Kirkby (one, the 90, operating from the latter to St Helens). A joint service between Liverpool and Wigan was operated by St Helens and Wigan corporations and Ribble – but Liverpool Corporation did not take part. However, Liverpool provided a substantial number of bus services to and within the adjacent borough of Bootle (in co-operation with Ribble) but then Bootle was so physically 'enjoined' to Liverpool that it would be difficult for the visitor to realise that he had left one and entered the other – or vice versa.

Given the geographical shape of Liverpool (with the city centre hugging the waterfront, and the inner districts and suburban areas fanning out to form a half-oval of just over 40 square miles), the corporation also operated an extensive number of orbital bus services (as it had done with trams). These provided convenient connections with radial services, thus providing citizens with the option of a number of cross-town travel patterns that did not require unnecessary journeys to and from the city centre.

Liverpool was by far the largest of the three corporation fleets which passed into the care of the new Merseyside Passenger Transport Executive in December, 1969, and with the other two (Birkenhead and Wallasey) physically separated by the wide Mersey, local identify was maintained, at least in the sense of livery. This continued when the St Helens and Southport fleets were joined to the PTE in 1974 and green became the standard colour for the entire fleet. However with the name 'Liverpool' banished from the buses and the coat of arms with its famous Liver Bird replaced by a nondescript logo, some of the city's sense of being was lost.

St Helens, Liverpool's neighbour to the east, was, by contrast, a smallish but expansionist operator and this took its buses far beyond the town whose name they displayed.

This authority was a latecomer to municipal transport, the corporation not exercising its right to take over the local company-owned tramway system until October 1919. Having just acquired its own trams, St Helens was keen to expand and the first corporation bus services – introduced during 1921/22 – were actually operated to act as substitutes for proposed tram services whose tracks were being laid. The first two permanent motorbus services were launched in 1923.

St Helens began operating trolleybuses in 1927; a second service followed two years later and in 1931 the corporation launched a joint trolleybus service with Lancashire United to Haydock, Ashton, Hindley and Atherton – a distance of almost 14 miles. By 1939, trolleybuses made up 57 per cent of the total bus fleet although they accounted for an even bigger proportion of overall mileage.

During the 1930's the motorbus system was greatly extended to take in new housing developments but St Helens also made extensive movements into neighbouring urban areas, which though relatively heavily populated, were not large enough to support municipal transport systems of their own. As a result, over time, St Helens Corporation Transport developed an 'interurban' system, with services to Liverpool, Warrington, Manchester and, the longest of all, to Southport (a full 30 miles).

The expansion of the system was reflected in a need to introduce service numbers, which took place in 1942, although initially these were confined to trolleybuses.

The trolleybus network looked secure with the appointment as manager, in 1949, of R Edgely Cox, who was a strong supporter of the wired electric vehicles. However, in a frank report to the transport committee in 1951, Mr Cox pointed out that if St Helens wanted to retain trolleybuses, substantial sums would need to be spend on renewing wiring and other vital ancillary equipment. After some debate, the corporation decided on a trolleybus abandonment scheme, which was completed by 1958.

Mr Cox was also remembered for bringing an order of 40 new, London Transport-type AEC RT's to St Helens, the only occasion a municipality purchased this vehicle straight from the factory rather than second hand from the capital.

St Helens passenger numbers peaked in 1955/56 (about five years later than the national average), when just over 50 million were carried on corporation buses. After that there was the familiar story of falling passenger numbers, rising costs and staffing difficulties, caused by competition from the many factories in full production at the time, although the introduction of one-man operation in 1967 helped alleviate the situation somewhat.

St Helens livery was a balanced mixture of red and cream, although its buses are probably best remembered for the branding used during the late 1940's, 1950's and early 1960's; this involved the words ST HELENS CORPORATION in large letters in an impressive art

THE CORPORATION BUS

deco setting, and placed on both sides of the lower panels. Sadly, the vehicles were eventually be given the corporate all over green livery of Merseyside Transport with its bland logo – progress or what?

If Eastbourne could lay claim to the first continuous municipal bus service in Britain, and the world, then 250 miles to the north, **Widnes** has claimed to have operated the first covered top municipal double deck buses in the country – and "probably" the world.

However, covered tops were a necessity rather than a luxury in a town with a large number of chemical factories, which spilled out 'acid rain', long before the term became common usage.

Widnes, now in Cheshire but until 1974 in Lancashire, was probably the largest town in the northwest of England not to have been served by trams, therefore the corporation bus made an early appearance - on Good Friday, 9 April 1909 with four Commer buses with solid tyres operating between the old Transporter Bridge at West Bank and Peelhouse Lane. The service was soon extended to Halton View, Farnworth and the Black Horse. Later, services were extended to Rainhill.

Services to most parts of Widnes began during the 20's and 30's so that by the outbreak of world war two an extensive network covered most of the town. A main line service operated every 10 minutes from the Transporter Bridge through the town and diverting at Deacon Road into several splinter services. However at no time during its existence did the undertaking use numbers or even letters to identify routes or services.

Widnes Corporation shared in the early post-war boom and in addition to the usual commercial and leisure passenger loadings, the department's buses were leased by factories such as Everite and even the new Ford Factory at Speke.

With the opening of the new Runcorn - Widnes Bridge in 1961, regular bus services were extended to Runcorn High Street Bus Station. Under the legislation then prevailing Widnes enjoyed the sole right to carry local passengers across the bridge, given that the previous bridge replaced had been owned by the corporation. Crosville Services in the Widnes area had restrictions on their ability to carry local passengers, including higher fares on Crosville buses and a payment to Widnes Corporation for each passenger that Crosville carried.

In 1966 one-man operation commenced on various routes, although the majority of new deliveries continued to be the now traditional East Lancs bodied Leyland Titan PD2 double-decker with 65 seats. The department took delivery of the first Leyland National for a municipal operator in 1971.

On local government reorganisation, Widnes became part of a wider district and the undertaking – officially Widnes Corporation Motor Omnibus Department – closed and metamorphosed as Halton Borough Transport.

Thus the Widnes name and coat of arms were lost but there was at least one improvement – numbers being introduced on 'town' services for the first time.

The first, petrol engine, buses to be operated by **Warrington** entered service in 1913 but the corporation continued to pin its faith in expanding the tramways and it was not until 15 years later that any new buses were purchased.

However the bus system quickly grew and by 1935 the trams were gone, after 225 million passenger journeys had been made since 1902 – with just one fatality.

Joint services across the town were established with Lancashire United Transport in 1940 and ten years later passenger demand peaked at 39 million in a single year.

At the start of the 1960's the fleet numbered around 80 vehicles, almost all being double-deckers. Livery was red and white although maroon and ivory had been used for a short period after world war two.

The first rear engine buses went into service in 1963 and one-man operation (on single-deckers) was introduced two years later; this was extended to double-deckers in 1970.

In 1974 Warrington was moved from Lancashire to Cheshire (administratively by the bureaucrats but perhaps not in the hearts of the local people) but the undertaking remained in municipal ownership and at the time of writing is one of the few still in council hands, operating under the trading name, Network Warrington.

Although the corporation bus, by its very name, was 'publicly owned', pride in municipal undertakings were just as great in Conservative-run towns as they were in Labour-held ones.

Nowhere was this more apparent than affluent, and somewhat genteel, **Southport**, on the Lancashire coast, where the immaculately turned out fleet was deemed to not just cater for passengers but to represent the intensely felt local civic pride.

Southport operated its first buses in 1924; up to 1930, the fleet had been restricted to a modest 12 vehicles but after that bus operation accelerated and the trams were gone by 1934.

With the onset of world war two, the Government transferred several Ministries to Southport for the duration, and the fleet, 45 strong in 1936, had been expanded to 63 by 1946. Even in 1951, with things back to number, the corporation boasted 78 vehicles, which coped with a passenger-carrying peak, that year, of 30 million.

In 1946, the corporation introduced a number of open-top sea-front services with locally constructed 23-seat bodywork, some of which were used exclusively for the beach service to Sandhills and Ainsdale.

By 1966 passenger numbers had declined to 15 million, about half of those carried in 1951, which inevitably led to the beginning one-man operation. Neverthless, Southport remained a superb compact undertaking with a simple service numbering system, which read: 1 Woodvale to Blowick; 2 Lord Street to Marshside; 3 Monument Square to Botanic Gardens; 4 Chapel Street to Halsall Road; 5 Chapel Street to Haig Avenue; 6 Monument Square to Blowick; 7 Monument Square to Russell Road; 8 Chapel Street to Carr Lane; 9 Lord Street to Crossens; 10 Lord Street to Crossens; 11 Lord Street to Woodvale; 12 Lord Street to Ainsdale; 13 Lord Street to Ainsdale Beach; 14 Lord Street to Liverpool Road; 15 Lord Street to Clive Road; 16 Lord Street to Guildford Road; 17 Lord Street to Balmoral Drive; 18 Lord Street to Everard Road; 19 Lord Street to Golf House; 20 Eastbank Street Square to Kew. As can be seen, many services terminated at Lord Street, the magnificent main thoroughfare and sometimes described as Southport's own *Champs Elysees*.

In 1974, to the fury of many local citizens, Southport was forced into the new metropolitan county of Merseyside rather than becoming a district in its own right within Lancashire. To add insult to injury it was enjoined, within Merseyside, with industrial Bootle to form the metropolitan borough of Sefton.

This, of course, meant Southport Corporation Transport being subsumed within Merseyside PTE and very soon the distinctive local livery of red and cream was replaced by Liverpool green. Local pride was revived for a period in the 1990's after Merseyside PTE was privatised and its successor operated local services under the fleetname 'Southport & District' and even brought back the old corporation colour scheme. Unfortunately, S&D was later sold to Arriva who had the vehicles repainted in corporate livery and branding and the individuality on which Southport prided itself was lost again.

Birkenhead was by far Cheshire's largest municipal transport undertaking but the town was better known for the building of ships and as the location for Britain's first street tramway, This took a route between Woodside Ferry and Birkenhead Park and was inaugurated by the ironically named American, George Francis Train, in 1861.

The bus did not make an appearance until 1905 when the Mersey Railway Company began running a feeder service to its railway stations serving Liverpool but this was successfully challenged by Birkenhead Corporation in the courts and the service ceased in 1907.

Twelve years later the corporation began a motorbus service of its own using five Leyland single-deckers. Initial bus livery was maroon and cream (the livery of the corporation trams) but this was later changed to a foam blue and cream to distinguish corporation services from those of Crossville, which at the time also used maroon.

The bus network extended generically but attempts to serve districts outside the boundary were challenged by Crossville, although the two operators eventually declared a truce and introduced a joint services agreement. A separate joint services deal was agreed with neighbouring Wallasey Corporation and this survived until the simultaneous closure of the two municipal undertakings.

Corporation trams still predominated in Birkenhead up to 1925 but after that an abandonment programme was put in place and this was completed in 1937.

Following the end of world war two and into the 1950's, services to serve new housing estates like Woodchurch and Pinkerton were launched. In 1955 the official name of the undertaking was changed to Birkenhead Municipal Transport.

Similar services were operated in their own groups, which by 1960 had elevated the numbers used to 99. To the uninitiated, this made the operation somewhat larger than it actually was in practice yet the system was extensive and covered the northern half of the Wirral Peninsula, serving areas outside the boundary such as Seacombe, New Brighton, Heswall and Port Sunlight. Circular workings also featured largely in the route network.

Different numbers were used for short workings, so that services 63 and 65, for example, were simply truncated versions of service 64. No less than 26 services converged on Woodside Ferry, 27 on the Town Hall, and 24 on Birkenhead Central Station. Indeed, some of those were operated specifically to tie in with the electric commuter trains which operated between various parts of Birkenhead and Liverpool city centre, via the Mersey railway tunnel.

Despite the financial and social pressures to introduce one-man operation, Birkenhead remained true to the half-cab bus, in fact up to 1968. Therefore when the fleet was absorbed into Merseyside PTE in late 1969, most of the 220-strong fleet still consisted of 'traditional' vehicles.

In most cities and towns that boasted a municipal undertaking, the core of the network was a recognised central area, from which services radiated.

A rare exception was **Wallasey**, next to Birkenhead, which was formed from a number of neighbouring but independent small towns and villages and did not become a county borough until 1910.

This situation led to a somewhat fragmented service pattern yet there was still a point on which most were concentrated – the Seacombe ferry terminal, from where ferries to Liverpool left every ten minutes.

Seacombe Ferry was the turning point for the first bus service (to Harrison Drive) in 1920 and further services mushroomed throughout the twenties as the tram track deteriorated. The last tram service ended in 1933. In the same year a new ferry terminal building and bus station was opened at Seacombe, which included a covered walkway that allowed passengers to transfer from bus to boat, and vice versa, without getting wet. Services were timed precisely to arrive and leave to coincide with the ferry timetable and it has been known for as many as 15 Wallasey Corporation buses to leave the terminal simultaneously, all on the blast of an inspector's whistle.

During the mid-thirties two bathing pools (one built to Olympic size standard) were opened and the promenade extended, and even more visitors flocked to Wallsey, and in particular its holiday resort of New Brighton, boosting the coffers of the transport department. As a result, fares went down progressively until

1935, from when they remained static for the following 15 years.

Livery was officially 'sea green', although to some eyes it may have appeared cream and to others, yellow.

The return of peace brought even greater demand from visitor traffic and the late forties and early fifties can be seen as the golden age of Wallasey Corporation Transport, with passenger numbers reaching almost 36 million in 1949/50. Apart from the seasonal traffic, there was an expansion of services for local residents to the Leasowe and Moreton areas and a reworking of joint services with Birkenhead Corporation.

Inevitably, leisure tastes changed, and visitors started to go further afield, which accelerated the decline of New Brighton as a resort. A steep reduction in the population of densely packed Liverpool also took its toll, as did the increase in car ownership among local Wallasey residents.

This led to the usual higher fares and cut backs in services, which further accelerated passenger decline (down to 14.8million in 1968/69), although in retrospect it is difficult to decipher what alternatives were open to management, here as elsewhere.

In 1958 Wallasey entered the record books when it became the first municipal undertaking in the country to introduce the rear engine Leyland Atlantean, although it seemed incongruous that these vehicles were branded with the somewhat dated fleet name – Wallasey Corporation Motors (with 'Motors' set in a semi-circle beneath the coat of arms). Later deliveries sported only the coat of arms but, of course, even this disappeared in 1969 when the undertaking was incorporated into the new Merseyside PTE.

Further into the heart of Cheshire county, **Chester** City Transport began the pre-war era with a new livery – maroon and cream. This was kicked off in March 1946 after Crossvile Motor Services decided to swap from maroon and cream to Tilling green, which was not dissimilar to Chester at the time.

Post-war service developments included the re-routing of the Town Hall to Rake & Pikel service via Sandy Lane, which allowed for the operation of double-deckers at all times and in December 1948 the General Station to Christleton route was extended to Littleton. In November 1949 a new service from the Town Hall to Blacon commenced. A single-deck service was introduced in October 1952 between the Town Hall and the Blacon Avenue junction of Ludlow Road, which operated under the low bridge on Blacon Hall Road.

In 1953 there was a complete renumbering of the service listings as follows: 1, General Station – Blacon & Saughall; 2, Town Hall-Ludlow Road, Blacon; 3, General Station – Christleton via St. Anne St., Town Hall and Stocks Lane; 4, Curzon Park (Earlsway) – Christleton and Littleton; 5, Christleton (Trooper Inn) – Saltney (Ring Road); 6, Vicars Cross – Saltney (Ring Road); 7, Town Hall – Cliveden via Hough Green; 8, Town Hall – Cliveden via Lache Lane; 9, General Station – Eccleston Avenue via Handbridge; 10, General Station – Eccleston and Cadet School, Eaton Hall; 11, General Station – Grove Avenue via Hoole Lane; 12, General Station – Grove Avenue via Tarvin Road; 13 Town Hall – Rake & Pike. This simplified the earlier list of service numbers, which had ranged from 1 to 26.

During 1957, when the number of vehicles operated stood at around 50, the undertaking's name was changed from Chester Corporation Transport to Chester City Transport.

Remarkably, Chester City Transport survived as an arm's length company for 22 years after deregulation in 1986, eventually succumbing to a takeover by First Group in 2007.

Stockport introduced trolleybuses in 1913 with a service between Mersey Square and Offerton.

The system used was not successful, however, the usual problems of early trolleybuses being compounded by Stockport having adapted the German Lloyd Kohler overhead system which comprised two wires of vertical overhead; there was only a single line of overhead so that when two trolleys going in the opposite direction met, one was forced to de-pole.

Not surprisingly, the last trolleybuses ran in 1919, the year that also saw the introduction of motorbuses, initially single-deckers but double-deckers followed in 1934. The service then began to spread out but not as widely as in similar sized towns because Stockport councillors remained very much faithful to their trams. However after the demise of the trams new bus services were launched to growing suburbs, such as Woodhall Estate in 1957 and Bridge Hall Estate in 1960. In 1967 a new joint service to Manchester via Green End and Kingsway commenced.

The hub of transport in Stockport was Mersey Square – dominated in those days by the giant edifice that was the Plaza cinema - because not only was this the main town centre terminal point but it also housed the corporation garage and offices for most of the existence of the undertaking. The square was also a sea of red because in addition to Stockport Corporation Transport this was the main colour sported by buses of the North Western Road Car Company, who not only operated many medium distances from the town but were based there as well. Added to this were red service providers of the likes of Manchester Corporation, Ribble and Midland Red.

By the early 1960's the fleet had grown to 170 buses, 22 of which were single-deck. Stockport Corporation buses had reputation for being superbly maintained and finished. This was a legacy from the tramway system, which came out of world war two almost as large as when hostilities started. Stockport track was still in relatively good condition and buses only gradually took over the bulk of the tram system, which survived until August 1951. Indeed it was the decision by Manchester – with whom Stockport had a joint service – which influenced the latter to do away with trams completely.

In addition to keeping their buses looking smart, the corporation had a reputation for squeezing several more years of useful service, beyond that of other operators, from its vehicles. This made Stockport a Mecca for enthusiasts because of the possibility of seeing 'vintage' buses still in passenger service. Perhaps unsurprisingly, Stockport boasted the last new front-engine buses of any municipal undertaking and all services were still being operated by conductors when the fleet was absorbed by SELNEC in 1969.

The **Stalybridge, Hyde, Mossley and Dukinfield** Transport and Electricity Board had the dubious distinction of the most cumbersome title in the municipal transport sector, being a joint operation by four textile towns.

They were unusual in that two of the towns straddled Cheshire and Lancashire, although the majority of the undertaking's activities was in Cheshire. Service buses were registered in Cheshire County Council.

Buses were launched in 1925 and in 1938 SHMD also constructed overhead wiring in Stalybridge although the undertaking never owned trolleybuses and this was used by Ashton and Manchester until 1966.

The livery was an attractive mid green and the coat of arms of all four constituent owners was displayed jointly on the lower side panels.

4

Lancashire South-East

Centre of the universe

If there was such a thing as the 'centre of the universe' during Britain's municipal bus heyday then it was surely the Piccadilly Gardens area of central Manchester.

For shoppers and office workers, the flower beds, shrubs and open green space provided a welcome respite from the busy city streets but what drew bus enthusiasts to Piccadilly was the red-liveried vehicles of Manchester Corporation, the green of neighbouring Salford, the blue of Ashton-under-Lyne, and a wide array of other examples from municipal fleets (some of them beyond Lancashire) who operated services to and from there

For such enthusiasts, this 'municipal transport rainbow' was as near as it got to perfect, especially as the Manchester undertaking was in its own right a premier league player – the third largest operator after Birmingham and Glasgow and boasting around 1,500 vehicles at its high water mark.

Manchester launched its first corporation bus service as early as 1906 but growth was fleeting and it was not until the early 1920's that purchasing began in earnest.

The growth in buses was accelerated by the appointment in 1929 of the then Edinburgh general manager, Stuart Pilcher, who was a tramwayman by training and sentiment but would not allow that to stand in the way of progress. He actually designed a lightweight tram for his new employers but when experiments also showed that buses performed better than trams on the heavily loaded 53 circular tram route, serving the vast Trafford Park industrial estate, (the buses knocked 11 minutes off a tram journey time of 53 minutes) abandonment of the latter began in earnest.

Pilcher wanted an all-motorbus system but against his will was forced by councillors to introduce trolleybuses in 1938, partly because they wanted to use home-grown coal and partly because…well…almost everyone else was developing trolleybuses so why shouldn't Manchester?

Trolleybus services were extended even after Pilcher's departure at the end of world war two but they always remained peripheral to the network as a whole. In mileage terms, the trolley system was fairly large but there were no cross-city routes. Services terminated in the city centre (at Piccadilly, Aytoun Street and Stevenson Square) and these were confined to the joint routes into Cheshire with Ashton and to parts of north-west Manchester. Although the corporation was still taking delivery of new trolleybuses in 1955, a decision to abandon was also made in that year. The last service closed on New Year's Eve, 1966.

A major event, albeit an aesthetic one, occurred in 1936 with the introduction of a 'streamline' design for buses, in which the primary red background colour was complimented by large curved 'wings' in white. This

THE CORPORATION BUS

design reflected the art deco architecture of the period and though it may look dated now, was considered the height of modernity at the time.

A year after the end of world war two, Manchester introduced its first buses with power doors and four years later advertising was permitted on upper panels for the first time.

Meanwhile, the last tram left for the depot in January 1949 – ironically the year that passenger usage within the undertaking as a whole reached its peak (492 million journeys).

In 1957 life was made easier for passengers with the erection of 170 ft. long shelter in Albert Square. In 1958 Chorlton Street bus station was opened, as was a rebuilt Piccadilly Bus Station, which was 577 ft. long, and 28 ft. wide with two-storey building containing Information Office and employee canteen.

A City Circle service was introduced in 1961 but, as with other cities who experimented in this manner, the route was largely unsuccessful and was withdrawn in 1964. In 1967, in anticipation of widespread one-man operation, fares were simplified to sixpence, one shilling or one and six (3p, 5p and 1.3p.) The first one- man operation of double deck vehicles began in August 1967.

At the start of the 1960's listed services (including peak hour and limited stop) numbered 2 to 139 (with few numbers unused), then from 150 to 162, then finally there was a somewhat isolated number 500 (limited stop between the city centre and Alderley). There were, in addition, five trolleybus services numbered in the '200' series.

The service map reflected the somewhat unconventional 'portrait' (as opposed to landscape) physical shape of Manchester. Approximately one-third of route mileage was beyond the boundary and the Manchester bus could be seen as far away as Buxton in Derbyshire and Biddulph in Staffordshire, almost in Stoke on Trent.

A large proportion of services left from and terminated at various city centre boarding points, over 30 from the recently-rebuilt Piccadilly bus station. Other extensively used central terminal points were Piccadilly north side, Stevenson Square, Chorlton Street, Albert Square and Cross Street (Royal Exchange).

Throughout its existence, livery used by the Manchester undertaking was red, initially with a large amount of white relief, although necessary cost cutting meant that this was eventually confined to an all over red.

With the passing of the Transport Act in 1968, Manchester's days as an independent municipal operator were numbered. However, the undertaking went out in a blaze of glory when its innovative penultimate manager, Ralph Bennett, launched the Mancunian. Introduced to the public on 1 April, 1968, this double-decker, rear engine bus had a simplified but sleek exterior design perfectly at ease with the mores of the time. The interior was also highly modernistic and included an American-style 'Johnson' fair box.

A prevalence of white over red in the colour scheme made the vehicle even more striking and its launch caused a sensation, although one half of the city's football fans may have been less impressed with the new fleet name – Manchester City Transport (actually City, rather than United, were the more successful of the two clubs at the time although that no doubt was pure coincidence!). Previously buses had carried the legend, 'City of Manchester' on the lower panels, with the coat of arms located directly above.

THE CORPORATION BUS

On 1 December, 1969, the corporation fleet became the largest single constituent part of the new SELNEC (South East Lancs North East Cheshire) Passenger Transport Executive and Manchester buses, like those of nine neighbouring authorities, lost their unique identity.

Before local government reorganisation a body of opinion in Manchester held that if only **Salford** would merge with "the city that made it" then Manchester, and not Birmingham, would be able to declare itself Britain's second city both in terms of acreage and population.

Certainly, within the field of passenger transport, the merged fleets of Manchester and Salford, would have knocked Birmingham off its perch as the largest municipal bus undertaking in Britain. With more than 300 buses at its peak, Salford was the third largest municipal operator in Lancashire, after Manchester and Liverpool.

The physical relationship between the two cities is certainly unusual, perhaps unique, in Britain, with the Salford boundary literally paralleling much of Manchester city centre; indeed before Dr Beeching's cuts to the railway system during the mid-1960's, one of Manchester's four principal railway terminals, Exchange, was officially not in Manchester at all but in Salford.

But living in the shadow of a world city like Manchester probably made Salfordians even more conscious of their own separate civic identity than might otherwise have been the case. And perhaps the most prominent outward sign of that identity was Salford's own municipal transport undertaking.

Salford introduced buses in 1920 and built up a modern fleet over the next two decades to gradually replace the tram system, although the last service did not run until 1947.

Unfortunately, Salford buses did not have a 'good war' and they emerged from the conflict as battered and bruised as some of our main industrial cities. However the situation was soon to change with the appointment, as general manager, of Charles Baroth, who arrived from Newport Corporation in 1946. He set about not only replenishing the fleet stock but ordered improved driving standards and stricter adherence to maintenance and repair procedures, all of which resulted in the undertaking regaining a pride that had been lacking for some years.

The new broom began his sweep by changing the fleet name from Salford Corporation to Salford City Transport. He also changed the colour scheme from red (assumedly to distinguish Salford further from Manchester) to an attractive mid-green with generous cream relief and new stops and other street furniture was erected. In the first 12 months of the Baroth era 40 per cent of the fleet had been painted in the new colours. He also resisted – unlike most other municipal managers - growing pressure to allow external advertising and helped prevent this by having the coat of arms placed on the upper panels. Only in 1968 – three years after Mr Baroth retired – did Salford finally allow advertising on its bus upper decks.

The programme of fleet renewal meant that Salford did not need to purchase one new vehicle between 1953 and 1962.

Relations with Manchester (which had been somewhat cool in preceding years) also improved; the two cities began a joint service, the 57/77 loop serving Reddish, Swinton and Pendlebury, in 1951 and four years later a cross-towns service, the 95/96 between

THE CORPORATION BUS

Whitefield in Salford and East Disbury in Manchester. Salford also operated longer distance services to Warrington, Bolton, Leigh, Wigan and Liverpool.

As was the case with its neighbour, Salford latterly had to economise on painting methods, which reduced the cream relief on panels, making the buses virtually all-green and somewhat drab. Yet there can be no doubting that for two decades from 1946, Salford boasted a superbly maintained fleet which served the citizens well in their daily lives – and highlighted the city's determination to show its separate identity from Manchester.

Bolton was by far the largest town in the old County of Lancashire and consequently boasted the largest municipal bus fleet after the cities of Manchester, Liverpool and Salford.

After a brief flirtation with steam and petrol-driven buses in the early 1900's, corporation bus services finally took off in 1923 with a service to Lower Street. There were still only three services at the beginning of 1925 but the bus network mushroomed the following year and its success signalled the beginning of the end of the tramway system, even though extensions to the tracks had been made up to 1924.

This was followed by involvement with neighbouring municipalities, as well as Lancashire United Transport, on a number of interurban express services. At around the same time the corporation also made its peace with Ribble with regard to the company's activities around Bolton.

In the early 1930's Bolton also became an owner of four trolleybuses, but these were operated by (and appeared in the livery of) South Lancashire Transport, whose wires reached the town in 1933. The agreement lasted until 1957.

By this time a decision to abandon the entire tramway system had been agreed but, as happened elsewhere, the plan was curtailed by world war two and it was not until 1947 that the final tram service, to Tonge Moor, closed.

Bolton's buses – with their dignified maroon and cream livery – were gaining a good reputation for external appearance but there was controversy in 1951 when upper panel advertising was introduced – or rather reintroduced. Some councillors were totally opposed while others agreed, providing advertisements for alcohol products and gambling were not permitted. However as costs rose and passenger numbers fell, opposition gradually became more muted.

As the 1960's dawned, Bolton had the biggest non-city municipal fleet in the country with nearly 280 buses, the vast majority of them double-deckers. This put it at 17th in the municipal pecking order – just two places behind Salford.

At that time bus routes were listed chronologically from 1 to 65, with just a few breaks, then 122, 215, 225, B15, B25, B35 X66 (Blackburn to Manchester). A number of services were operated jointly with Ribble, LUT and Bury, Leith and Salford corporations.

Although Bolton Corporation Transport, like so many others, was not to survive the new decade, the sixties certainly opened it with a bang, principally in the person of the new manager, Ralph Bennett, who had arrived after a two-year stint as manager at Great Yarmouth. Although an engineer, he was as interested in the design of buses as well as their mechanical function and he co-operated with various coachbuilders to improve both the look and function of the new rear-engine double-deckers then coming into service. This included the installation of translucent fibre glass panels which brought new light, and increased sense of space, the upper decks – as well as making a bus look 'sexy' and helping it, to some extent, to make up some ground lost to the private car.

At Bolton overall bus appearance was enhanced by an increase in the amount of cream in proportion to the overall body. However, maroon was still used in large measure, maintaining the dignity of 'Bolton Transport', the fleetname, which was placed between the municipal coat of arms on the lower side panels.

Unfortunately Mr Bennett was poached by 'big brother' Manchester in 1965 but he had set the tone for the few remaining years of the undertaking, until Bolton Corporation Transport became part of SELNEC North and the famous maroon and cream that marked the town's separate identity was replaced by corporate-regional garish orange.

Little **Leigh** had never been a tramway operator, so began its own motorbus operation as early as 1920.

By 1940 the fleet had grown to 40 vehicles but this doubled in size during hostilities because of the need to service the Risley Royal Ordnance Factory. After the war the fleet numbers dropped back to just over 50 and were at 61 in 1961.

In September 1957, the Leigh to Bolton trolleybuses of Lancashire United Transport were replaced by motorbuses, with the new service (No. 82) being operated jointly by Leigh and Bolton corporation and LUT, although Bolton's operational involvement was actually restricted to school journeys. The trolleybuses on the Leigh to Mosley Common route were also replaced by a new bus service (No. 84), which was operated jointly with LUT, although Leigh buses did not appear on the route until later.

The blue and white buses of Leigh became part of SELNEC in December 1969 and just over four years later Leigh itself disappeared when it was absorbed into the new, extended borough of Wigan.

After 21 years of tramways, **Bury** Corporation first used motorbuses on a service between the town centre and Walshaw, which was launched in September 1925, using one-man operated, 26-seater, single-deck Leylands.

During the next few years motor buses were used to provide new services to other parts of the area, including Ainsworth and Brandlesholme Road, which were not served by tramways. Development of new routes progressed steadily and inter-running arrangements were made with neighbouring operators. Before 1930 services were running through to Rawtenstall, Burnley, Rochdale, Manchester, Stockport, Farnworth, Bolton and Ramsbottom. Joint Services were also run with Ribble.

With the last tram having run in February 1949, buses were used to serve the new housing estates built during the 1950's, although overall passenger loadings actually began to diminish from 1951 (42 million passenger journeys had been made the previous year).

A major change to the service pattern took place in 1959 when some of the major routes that terminated in the central area were linked in pairs to provide cross-town facilities. This helped reduce congestion by

THE CORPORATION BUS

eliminating many of the bus turning operations formerly carried out in the town centre.

At the end of world war two, Bury's buses were painted red and cream. Then a decision was made to change this to green and cream, although the green was a lighter application than that used by Salford, when it too switched from red to green in 1947.

Immediately prior to closure, Bury Corporation Transport operated 27 routes numbered 1 to 38 and seven more numbered variously between 47 and 65.

Somewhat smaller than most other county borough undertakings around Manchester, Bury contributed around 100 vehicles to SELNEC when it replaced the various local corporations in 1969.

Originally, all **Ramsbottom** vehicles were single-deck because of the low height of the bridge at Stubbins railway station, but when the roadway was lowered underneath the bridge giving sufficient clearance for double-deck vehicles, the first of which arrived in late 1947.

Since 1949 Ramsbottom, Rawtenstall and Haslingden had shared the same general manager and obviously had considered forming a joint undertaking. However, when Rossendale Joint Transport Committee was finally formed in April 1968, Ramsbottom decided to remain independent with its dozen maroon and white buses, although this was short lived as the takeover by SELNEC was just 18 months away.

With its trademark gothic town hall, close to where many bus services terminated, **Rochdale** was a fiercely independent minded borough where opposition to absorption by SELNEC was particularly strong.

Corporation buses were inaugurated in 1926 and the success of the first double-deckers, which arrived four years later, spelled the end of the tramway system just two years after that, Rochdale being the first major municipal operator in Lancashire to go over completely to motorbuses. Growth was unspectacular but solid and there were services to Manchester, Oldham, Bury and Bacup in addition to the ever-expanding housing estates being developed by the expanding borough

A further expansion was the service to the new estate at Kirkholt, launched in January 1949, with further services to Mettle Cote and Wallbank following.

There were few changes after that and by the start of the 1960's the corporation had around 150 vehicles providing an established network of services in and around the borough. In 1952 the mileage travelled by the fleet was 4.350 million with approximately 60 million passenger journeys made.

Rochdale was an efficient, small- to medium-sized undertaking, which is reflected in its list of services from the early 1960's: 1 Castleton via Deeplish; 1a Castleton via Oldham Road; 3 Newhey, Rochdale, Littleborough, via Entwisle Road; 3a Newhey, Rochdale, Littleborough via John Street; 3b Birch Hill; 4 Norden, Manchester; 4 Rochdale, Bamford, via Mellor Street; 5 Rochdale, Bamford via Bury Road; 6 Newhey, Rochdale, Littleborough Summit or Stansfield via Entwisle Road; 6a Newhey, Rochdale, Littleborough Summit or Stansfield via John Street; 7 Healey, Rochdale, Wardle via Entwisle Road; 7a Healey, Rochdale, Wardle via John Street;

THE CORPORATION BUS

8 Hollingworth Lake, Shore, Stansfield or High Peak; 8 Rochdale, Hollingworth Lake; 8 Rochdale Manchester express; 9 Rochdale, Ashton; 9c Rochdale, Kirkholt Flats; 10 Syke, Rochdale, Turf Hill; 11a Kirkholt, Rochdale, Norden via Spotland Road; 11c Kirkholt, Rochdale, Norden via Mellor Street; 12a Low Hill, Rochdale, Daniel Fold or Lanehead; 14 Kingsway, Rochdale, Greave; 15 Rochdale, Shaw; 16 Rochdale, Bacup; 16 Rochdale, Wallbank; 17 Rochdale, Manchester; 17t Rochdale, Castleton via Tweedale Street; 18 Rochdale, Kirkholt; 19 Rochdale, Bury via Jericho; 20 Rochdale, Todmorden; 21 Rochdale, Bury via Heywood; 24 Rochdale, Royton, Manchester limited stop; 90 Rochdale, Royton, Manchester express.

As can be seen, 'Rochdale' was preferred to 'town centre' on destination screens – might we infer from this that Rochdale looked upon itself as the centre of a mini-metropolis?

For many years Rochdale buses carried streamline styling, which seemed to lend itself to the livery of mid to dark blue and cream. Towards the end of the life of the undertaking, however, cream became the dominant colour with blue reduced to providing the relief.

During the heyday of the undertaking, around 20 of the corporation's services terminated in the town centre, where the local cream and blue mingled with the more overall blue of Ashton, Manchester red, Bury Lincoln green, Todmorden olive green and Oldham maroon. Indeed, with this variety of operators and the proliferation of shelters, one might have imagined being not in Rochdale but in Manchester Piccadilly.

Oldham Corporation introduced buses as early as 1913 and by 1914 was operating three routes. However, the cotton town remained a tramway stronghold and buses were withdrawn in 1919, five years elapsing before their reintroduction.

A joint trolleybus service with Ashton began in 1925 but Oldham's involvement lasted just over a year. However the motorbus services continued to expand and from 1934 the run down of the tram system began although the last service was not closed until 1946.

Although there was the same post-war boom experienced elsewhere, passenger numbers peaked in the early 1950's and in 1953 the corporation succumbed to pressure to allow advertising on bus upper panels

White and maroon had been standard Oldham colours for many years but in 1963 a new manager, the former deputy Harry Taylor, experimented with a two-tone blue (medium and light) with yellow relief. Public reaction was hostile and the existing livery was retained, even though Mr Taylor's stated motive had been to cut down on repaint costs. Some years later the colour scheme became cream and pommard (a soft shade of red) with the coat of arms and the legend, COUNTY BOROUGH OF OLDHAM moved from the lower side panels to the front upper side panels. This livery looked particularly impressive on the new rear-engine Atlanteans coming on stream and was well received by the public this time.

In 1965 Oldham Corporation hit the transport headlines when a routine inspection by the Ministry of Transport found faults on almost 100 buses and many vehicles had to be hired from adjacent operators while the problems were put right. Mr Taylor blamed buying decisions by previous transport committees and a shortage of skilled craftsmen at the workshops.

One of the most significant changes to affect Oldham Corporation Transport was inaugurated just 18 months before the end of its existence. Since their inception, corporation buses had carried route letters, to distinguish them from the tram services then in operation. As the system became all-bus, 'main' arterial routes were given numbers but less frequent services feeding in from more outlying areas continued to be identified with letters. On 1 April 1968 numbers became the norm for all services. At the time service letters were A to H, M to P, S and T and V, with X given to depot workings, specials, etc. As for route numbers, these went from 1 to 14 without breaks then with several breaks to 24, 34, 56, 69, 98 and 153, all the latter mentioned numbers being used for joint workings with other operators.

The new integrated numbering system seemed to work well as there were little or no complaints from the general public. So, the corporation bus in Oldham went out on a reasonable 'high' after 56 years of service.

The corporation bus in **Ashton-under-Lyne** was, for many years, distinguishable by its 'royal' colour scheme of red, white and blue, made all the more distinctive by streamlining. However, in 1954 this was changed to a more sedate peacock blue with white.

Introduced in 1923, motorbuses replaced trams between 1932 and 1938. The first new bus service after world war two was to Parkbridge and in 1950 a new route to Rayner Lane Estate (Crowhill) was opened, with services being re-organised on a cross-town basis.

LANCASHIRE SOUTH-EAST

By 1955 the fleet consisted of 21 trolleybuses and 50 motorbuses, the former being worked as a joint service between Ashton and Manchester with Manchester Corporation

By now, however, Manchester Corporation was considering abandonment of trolleybuses and in July 1960 the final Ashton trolleybus ran to Haughton Green but another four years elapsed before the next trolleybus route (to Manchester via Guide Bridge) was converted to motorbus operation.

A new bus station was opened in November 1963 and many of the former Market Square termini were moved there, although, because of the cost of new overhead, trolleybus services did not use it. The closure of Ashton's trolleybuses coincided with those of Manchester, on 31 December 1966.

In January 1967 the last new bus route to be opened by Ashton Corporation was to the new housing estate at Gambrel Bank, just under two years before the municipal fleet was absorbed by SELNEC.

Having launched its first electric trams in 1901, **Wigan** waited 18 years before launching a motorbus service and it was not until 12 years after that (1930) that a second service was introduced.

In the meantime, Wigan also became a trolleybus operator in 1925, one of four undertakings to launch the electric system in that year. There was only one service, from the Market Place to Hartland Hill via Springfield but this looked likely to expand greatly when, in 1930, there was a proposal to replace the tram network with trolleybuses. However, motorbuses were eventually chosen and the last tram ran in the spring of 1931. In the autumn of the same year Wigan replaced its 'fleet' of trolleybuses – which only ever numbered four – with motorbuses.

It was perhaps, just as well, that the Wigan trolley fleet remained so small because throughout their six short years of life, Wigan did not actually have legal authority to operate trolleybuses!

Wigan gradually developed an extensive network of town and district 'regular' motorbus services, numbering in excess of 50, plus at least 14 works services. There were also long distance services to Bolton, Liverpool, St Helens and Salford (although the latter actually said 'Manchester' on the destination screen). Many services had several terminal points and letter suffixes were common. Incidentally, Wigan must have contained the most unsettling destination screen in the country – 'Dangerous Corner'.

At its peak the fleet numbered more than 150 vehicles, the vast majority being double-deckers. Wigan Corporation also had a reputation for superb maintenance and upkeep of its vehicles, a fact reflected in the refusal to permit external advertising right to the very end – this enabled the coat of arms often to be displayed to best effect on the upper side panels.

Wigan initially escaped the clutches of SELNEC in 1969 but became part of Greater Manchester PTE when Wigan and its environs were incorporated within the new metropolitan county in April 1974 – and the magnificent crimson and white livery was gradually substituted by regional burnt orange.

Looking at the map, Wigan appeared to be squeezed between Greater Manchester and the other metropolitan county of Merseyside and to the bureaucratic mind, it must have seemed tidier to lump in this ancient town (which goes back to Roman times) with one of the two metropolitan giants rather than allow it to stay in the truncated county of Lancashire. Had the latter taken place, Wigan would have retained local ownership of its buses for many more years – and may still have been in business today, just like nearby Warrington and Widnes (Halton).

5

Lancashire North

Barrow, Blackpool, and beyond

In 1960 Lancashire accounted for more than a quarter of all the UK's municipal bus undertakings so it is hardly surprising that in this respect the Palatinate was a county of two halves.

The south of the county was characterised by two municipal giants, Manchester and Liverpool, around which were clustered many more operators of various sizes in an overwhelmingly industrial and urbanised setting.

However, north of a line roughly stretching from Southport to Rochdale, the landscape was more rural, with bigger distances between urban communities, many of which retained a 'market town' atmosphere.

The most north-westerly operator of municipal buses in Lancashire, and therefore in England, was **Barrow**, a shipyard town which nevertheless stood on the edge of the Lake District. The corporation launched its first service in 1923 when trams were otherwise dominant. A small Ford vehicle was used for the route, which went from the Roose tram terminus to Rampside, followed shortly after by the purchase of two Chevrolet buses.

LANCASHIRE NORTH

Further extensions took place throughout the twenties and by 1932 the bus had completely replaced the tram, the ceremonial 'last tram' being driven by the same motorman who operated the first (horse-drawn) tram in 1885, almost half a century earlier. The impressive Prussian blue livery, which marked out Barrow buses, was also introduced around this time.

Two years later Barrow introduced route colour destination blinds – a feature that existed until the 1960's. Green was used for the Abbey to Biggar Bank route; blue for the Roose to Tea House route; red for the Hawcoat to Shore route and yellow for the Hawcoat to Harrel Lane route

In 1950 alterations were made to the Ormsgill to Harrel Lane and the Oxford Street to Risedale services to provide a circular service and double-deck vehicles were introduced; in 1953 the Ormsgill to Risedale service was extended to the new housing estate at Newbarns. In October 1958 one-man-operation was introduced on the Coast Road service to Ulverston. Fleet size at this time was around 60.

In its heyday Barrow Corporation was a very high volume carrier in daytime for such a small operator, because many of the thousands who worked at the Vickers shipyard preferred to take lunch at home.

However, the undertaking eventually experienced the same decline as many other smaller municipalities and in May 1989 – by which time it had become an arm's length company – Barrow Transport finally lost a protracted battle with Ribble and stopped trading.

Barrow was one of a cluster of three small municipal undertakings at the northern tip of Lancashire, around Morecambe Bay. Another was the town of **Morecambe** itself, which held a record in transport history, being the last municipal operator of horse trams on the British mainland; these reaching the depot (or should that be stable?) for the last time in 1926.

Morecambe had never operated electric trams but as early as 1919 launched its first bus service. Growth was fleeting at first but a big impetus for expansion came in 1929 with the amalgamation of the Borough of Morecambe and the adjacent Heysham Urban District Council, after which the new enlarged authority set up a network of services under the fleetname, 'Morecambe & Heysham Corporation'.

Morecambe shared a problem with other holiday destinations in that the fleet had to cope with two vastly different levels of demand between summer and winter. The problem here was confounded by the presence of a relatively small resident population, about one third of whom were beyond retirement age. Still, successive managers performed this balancing act remarkably well and in all its existence the undertaking never had to call on assistance from the rate fund, although a loss was recorded in its final year of operation. Passenger numbers peaked at almost 13 million in 1955.

The corporation managed to replace two thirds of its pre-war fleet between l945 and 1951 and the last of these vehicles was not taken out of service until 1978. One-man operation was introduced in 1967, and in the same year further expense was saved by using open-toppers for all services operating along the Promenade during summer, thus ending wasteful duplication between 'tourist' and 'town' traffic.

For most of its existence, Morecambe livery was a somewhat sombre mid green with little in the way of white relief, a colour scheme more at home in a grimier big city. However towards the end, the colours were reversed and in their last days Morecambe buses (by now mostly single-deckers) looked very attractive in white with a contrasting dark green band and skirting.

The undertaking's independent existence came to an end in 1974 when Morecambe & Heysham Corporation was absorbed into the new City of Lancaster District Council, whose area went far beyond the boundary of the city proper. However, for some years afterwards, local services remained much as before (i.e. concentrated within Morecambe and Heysham), although the buses sported a new blue livery and a new branding in the fleet-name of its near neighbour – ironic, given that Morecambe actually provided more vehicles to the new joint undertaking than did Lancaster.

Unlike Morecambe, **Lancaster** Corporation did operate electric trams but the system was small and closed in 1931 after less than three decades.

Regular bus operation began early, when, in 1916, the corporation became one of only three local authorities in the country to operate battery-electric buses. Five of these vehicles, manufactured by Edison, were purchased to provide services to a projectile factory on Caton Road. Although cheaper and more reliable than petrol-engine buses at the time, an inability to work on anything but short routes (before requiring a re-charge) made the battery electrics unprofitable. Petrol engine buses were operated from 1924 and double-deckers came on the scene in 1932.

In 1937 the corporation made a great stride forward in its administrative and operating capacity by acquiring a new office and departmental office, which was located on Kingsway, and a new central transport hub was created with the opening of Damside Bus Station. That same day saw the launch of a joint service with Ribble between Scotforth (on the southern extremity of Lancaster) and Higher Heysham (on the fringe of Morecambe and Heysham) but this became an early casualty of the war.

A quarter of a century later, Lancaster and Ribble revived this service, in part, with a new service between Morecambe Battery and the then new University of Lancaster but only some time after the Lancaster and Morecambe undertakings merged did meaningful development on joint services between the two towns begin.

Passenger usage peaked at just over 14 million in 1952 and afterwards Lancaster, like most other municipal operators, faced the challenge of rising costs and falling passenger numbers. Route numbers and initials were both tried; numbers were consecutive and the services operated settled at around 15.

In October 1973 a new one-way system was opened in the town centre. This caused some buses to double back in a loop in order to reach the appropriate boarding points, leading to the fleet clocking up an extra 50,000 miles a year. However, this was compensated for by a significant decrease in traffic congestion, and improved the level of timekeeping.

For many years ruby red with white was the livery of Lancaster buses but following the merger with Morecambe the primary colour became blue. Although the smaller of the two undertakings, only 'Lancaster' was retained on the new fleetname as this was the title given to the new district council into which the two towns were placed. At first the buses were given the dignified branding, 'Lancaster City Transport' but this was replaced by the somewhat unimaginative 'Lancaster City Council', a name that took the people-carrying buses down to the same level of dustcarts and other basic municipal vehicles.

The merger gave the new undertaking economies of scale and the situation was helped by an integrated services agreement with Ribble, which worked out at 55.45 bus miles in favour of the latter. This agreement, however, suffered from the consequences of deregulation and the undertaking eventually fell into the hands of Stagecoach in 1996.

In keeping with Lancashire's position as the centrepiece of municipal transport operation in this country, all four of the red rose county's famous seaside resorts – Blackpool, Lytham St Annes and Southport, in addition to Morecambe - boasted their own corporation buses.

The largest undertaking of them all both in actual and transport terms, **Blackpool** is most famous for its trams, being the first town in Britain to boast an electric tramway (in 1885) and the only one to continuously operate a tram service since then.

Blackpool, however, was also one of the more interesting motorbus operators too, not least in terms of origins. When, in July 1921, the corporation opened its first bus route, this was a two-mile service between the communities of Thornton and Cleveleys, both of which were actually outside the Blackpool borough boundary. This unusual event actually had its origins in a political dispute with one of the railway companies involving competition with the Fleetwood tram road. Therefore it was not until 1924 that corporation motorbus services within the borough boundary actually commenced – an inland service along Devonshire Road and a service along North Shore, the latter being a temporary tramway substitution as a result of track doubling.

However, further extension of bus services was slow, thanks in part to resistance within some factions of the council who saw this as a threat to the future of the entire tramway network, and consequently this allowed local private operators – one in particular – to steal a thunder on the corporation in serving new housing areas. Eventually the corporation – as happened in many places elsewhere – got round the problem by buying out its main competitor.

As the bus system began to grow, there came increasing clamour for service identification so numbers were introduced, the first series being numbered 1 to 9, although the isolated Thornton-Cleveleys service remained un-numbered.

Blackpool's legendary manager, Walter Luff, who arrived in 1932, is most famously associated with the resort's streamliner single-deck and 'balloon' double deck tramcars, but he was also responsible for the introduction of streamliner buses which made this undertaking, if not unique, at least highly unusual. These vehicles boasted sunroofs and had enclosed centre entrances and double stairs, which was believed to encourage quicker boarding and leaving by passengers and made it less likely that conductors would miss fares. What also made these buses so different were their fully-enclosed fronts (as opposed to the half-cabs found in most other cities and towns), which made them look like trolleybuses but without the booms. This led to a long love affair with full-cab fronts in Blackpool, which lasted even after central entrances were dispensed with in favour of open rear entrances.

This development marked out Blackpool buses as strikingly different from other municipal ones for the town's many visitors but another change by Mr Luff was probably just as significant for locals – the replacement of the livery from red and cream to green and cream, on the basis that this would differentiate corporation buses from those operated by the rival regional operator, Ribble. Increasingly over the years cream became the more dominant of the two colours.

After world war two, the tram system continued to be the main shifter of holidaymakers and day trippers but as Blackpool grew inland, additions to bus services were required and by 1953 the annual mileage had increased to 100,000. By 1956 service numbers were from 1 to 11, 13 to 18 and 22 to 25, with around half having A/B/C suffixes for short or seasonal workings. At one time the fleet size extended to over 160 vehicles, the majority double-deckers.

By 1963 the last 'street' tramway service had been withdrawn, with trams confined to the 11-mile Promenade route between Starr Gate and Fleetwood (with numerous short working services along the way). Since then Blackpool's buses have mainly catered for the local population, although even during their heyday, trams never reached the popular inland tourist attraction of Stanley Park, which was always served by buses.

Like all the municipal undertakings still in existence in 1986, Blackpool became an arm's length council-owned company and eight years later took over the neighbouring Flyde Borough undertaking. At the time of writing it remains in municipal ownership.

Always in the shadow of its giant neighbour, **Lytham St Annes** was, nevertheless, one of the more interesting of the smaller municipal operators. It's deep blue and cream livery contrasted sharply with that of Blackpool and seemed to emphasise the difference between the two – one big and brash, the other small and genteel.

The borough of Lytham St Annes was formed in 1922 and corporation buses were launched a year later.

In 1935, Lytham St Annes launched a joint service, route 11, with Blackpool Corporation, which ran from Adelaide Place, Blackpool to Lytham Square. In 1937, after the closure of its trams, Lytham, again with Blackpool, launched two more routes, 11A and 11B, both of which terminated in the heart of St Annes.

A local service within the joint borough was also operated and at their peak, fleet numbers grew to around 40.

At one time Blackpool Corporation offered to buy out the Lytham St Annes undertaking but was turned down. The issue came up again in 1982, by which time Lytham St Annes had become Fylde Borough. With both undertakings haemorrhaging money, Blackpool offered to increase its services to and within Fylde Borough to enable the latter's loss-making transport department to be closed down and to get it 'off the hook', so to speak. But local pride remained strong and by a small majority the council decided to reject the Blackpool offer and look for economies on its own.

Fylde Borough Transport (by now a limited company) was eventually sold to its employees in 1993 but Blackpool came back a third time and after negotiations returned the buses of Lytham St Annes to municipal ownership (albeit under the Blackpool name) the following year.

Municipal bus operation in **Preston**, the county town of Lancashire, began with a service from the Town Hall to the Plugington district in 1922 because the local roads were deemed incompatible for running trams.

This was meant to be a 'one off' and throughout 1922 Preston Corporation carried out an extensive renewal of the tramway permanent way, which survived intact until 1932 when buses, for the first time, started to replace tram routes. Surprisingly, total abandonment of the tram network was then achieved in two and a half years, the last service running in December 1935.

From very early on Preston buses were given a somewhat complicated route identification system. A few undertakings used letters rather than the more common numbers but in Preston some services were allotted more than one letter so that identification became an abbreviation of the destination itself. For example, Plugington was identified by PL, and Frenchwood by FR; on the eve of world war two, there were 16 services variously identified.

Matters were complicated further in 1948 when the corporation entered into a joint services agreement with Ribble and routes jointly operated were numbered P1 to P5 (extended a quarter of a century later to P7).

During the 1950's routes exclusively operated by the corporation began serving Cromwell Road (CR), Longsands Lane (LS) and Brookfield (BF).

In 1965 Preston took delivery of the last new buses in its traditional maroon and cream livery; in 1967 it was agreed to change to blue and ivory, although the process was not completed until 1971.

Meanwhile, traffic operations underwent a major change with the opening, in 1968, of the new Preston Bus Station, which at the time was said to be the largest in Europe. Corporation buses were allocated stands 1 to

40 and almost overnight the familiar concentration of bus shelters and stances – almost as much a part of the 'corporation bus scene' as the vehicles themselves, were removed from the town centre streets.

By 1974 the local authority was no longer allowed to call itself 'Preston Corporation', although this did little to affect the appearance of the buses as the title had fallen from use. However from then on 'Borough of Preston' appeared in fairly large script.

In 1980 the undertaking finally succumbed to modernity and the letters system of route identification was replaced by numbers - in this case 5 to 43, covering 26 services.

After deregulation in 1987 it was decided that changing the fleetname to 'Preston Bus' would be more in keeping with the times although one wonders what was wrong with emphasising the town's famous motto – 'Proud Preston'.

Blackburn had obtained authorisation to operate buses as early as 1908 but this was not taken up until July 1929 – and even then buses were intended only as feeders for the tramway system.

Eighteen months later the corporation changed direction and sought parliamentary powers to operate trolleybuses as replacements for its trams although; why this was never carried through remains something of a local mystery.

The following year the corporation purchased 12 new buses, which enabled it to take over local services provided by Ribble and the network was further expanded by the purchase of the privately-owned Blackburn Bus Company. The performance of the buses compared well with those of the municipal trams, especially as the latter were restricted by numerous sections of single track. Therefore in principle the decision was made to completely abandon the tramway system, although this was interrupted by world war two and, consequently, not completed until 1949.

A major physical change took place in 1954 when The Boulevard – the large waiting area at the front of Blackburn railway station – was reconstructed to accommodate buses. A year later a new service was launched to serve the Shadsworth Estate, this being extended three years later.

The 1954 timetable shows the following services operated: 1,2, Intack and Church; 3, Wilpshire; 5, Preston New Road; 8, Darwen (stopping); 9, Accrington (limited stop); 10, Wensley Fold; 11, Whitebirk; 12, London Road; 13, Mosley Street; 14, Little Harwood; 15, Darwen (limited stop); 16, Green Lane via Wellington Inn; 17, Green Lane via Fielding Crescent; 18,19; Feniscowles; 21, Moorgate; 22, Tockholes; 23, 24, Rivedge Circular; 25, Lammack; 26, Pleckgate; 27, Guide via Lower Darwen; 28, Guide via Haslingden Road; 29, Hoddlesden; 31, Queen's Park via Queen's Park Road; 32, Queen's Park via Lambeth Street; 33, Queen's Park Hospital; 36, Cherry Tree; 41, Pleasington Cemetery; 42, Higher Croft; 44, Shadsworth Hall; 45, Brownhill; 46, Accrington (stopping); 47, Filey Crescent.

There then followed a period of consolidation, with the fleet exceeding 100 vehicles.

One-man operation began in 1967, with the arrival of 45-seater Tiger Cub single-deckers and just over a year the double deck Atlantean was introduced to the fleet. Both these vehicle types carried a revised livery of cream with green – whereas before green had been the dominant colour.

THE CORPORATION BUS

With local government reorganisation in 1974, a new council, Blackburn with Darwen, emerged and the neighbouring **Darwen** fleet was incorporated into that of Blackburn.

Darwen Corporation had operated motorbus services from 1926 although the tramway system, albeit in decline, managed to survive for another 20 years – unusual for such a small municipal operator.

After world war two, several new services were launched and current ones extended to serve new housing estates, with Darwen Circus being the hub of the network. Although small, Darwen was a forward-thinking undertaking and the last open platform buses were ordered as early as 1955. By the early sixties the fleet stood at 50, eight of these being single-deckers.

For most of their existence, Darwen Corporation buses were painted red with cream relief, although in the latter years cream gradually become the dominant colour.

To cater for Darwen sensitivities, the roofs of all new and re-painted buses in the enlarged Blackburn fleet following the 1974 merger became red although over time the livery reverted to traditional Blackburn green and cream, albeit in various permutations.

To the outsider, **Accrington** is synonymous with the unusual name of the local football club, Accrington Stanley, which went bankrupt in 1962 but, miraculously, returned to the League more than 45 years later.

For the bus enthusiast, football took a second place to the daring and very distinctive livery of Accrington Corporation Transport – dark blue with medium red relief, the colours of the local East Lancs Regiment. For some it was just too garish but most liked it, and congratulated the Accrington management on its boldness when some of the bigger players in corporation bus-land played safe with reds or greens.

What made Accrington livery even more distinctive was the black colouring around the lower deck window panes – said to be in remembrance of the local volunteers, the 'Accrington Pals', who as part of the East Lancs, went over the top on the first day, 1 July, of the Battle of the Somme in 1916 and suffered more than 500 casualties. However, the connection has never actually been proven.

The first corporation buses ventured on to the streets of Accrington in 1928 and were so successful that the tramway system was closed within four years.

A good relationship was struck up with Ribble early on and remarkably this endured for many years. Not long after buses were launched, Accrington paid £2,250 for its share in the joint buyout, with Ribble, of a local private bus company and the corporation received a half share of the receipts of several local Ribble services thereafter.

Advertising was permitted on the upper deck panels from 1950 but, this being non-conformist territory, a ban on advertising alcoholic beverages was not lifted until 1959.

Immediately prior to local government reorganisation, Accrington Corporation operated 14 local services and eight longer-distance joint services, the latter in association with Bolton, Haslingden, Rawtenstall corporations and Ribble. In the early sixties, vehicle numbers stood at just under 50, about a quarter of them single-deckers.

The Accrington livery was retained when the bus fleet was taken over by the new Hyndburn district council in

1974. After this the vehicles carried the fleet name of the new authority – but to the majority of the local population they surely remained 'Accy' buses.

The three adjacent towns of **Burnley, Colne and Nelson** in the far north-eastern part of Lancashire operated their own corporation buses and trams until 1933 when a merger produced the BCN joint undertaking.

Nelson and Colne had first started operating motor-buses in 1923 and Burnley – by far the biggest of the three towns – followed suit a year later when five buses were delivered to start a route between Abel Street, Stoneyholme, the Centre and Towneley via Branch Road. Buses were found to be the cheapest and most efficient way of serving the new housing estates growing beyond the tram termini and the first double-deckers – 14 AEC Regents – were ordered in 1931.

The amalgamation took place on 1 April 1933 with approximately 100 buses and 70 trams, two-thirds of which were supplied by Burnley. The new manager was also the former Burnley chief, Charles Stafford.

The Burnley colour scheme of red and cream was also adopted although BCN was an early convert to increasing the element of cream on the panels, a policy not adopted until much later by most other undertakings.

Post-war the usual extensions were required to service booming factories and new housing estates.

Despite Burnley, Colne and Nelson being an integrated undertaking, services were set up in separate groups for each of the three towns - Colne Area, Nelson Area and Main Line (Burnley). Colne services, most of which set out from various stops in the town centre, ventured as far out as Keighley in Yorkshire.

Burnley Colne and Nelson was a keen buyer of single-deckers, this making up about one-fifth of the fleet at a time when double-deckers were still the preferred choice, even among smaller operators.

On local government reorganisation in 1974 Burnley became a district within Lancashire, while Colne and Nelson were merged to become the new district of Pendle. Subsequently, the undertaking from then on became Burnley & Pendle.

Situated in Lancashire, but almost on the Yorkshire border, **Haslingden** was another small undertaking, with some local services worked but the principle operation being the route between Accrington and Bacup.

In 1949, the general manager of **Rawtenstall** took over responsibility for Haslingden operations, although the fleets remained separate (the same manager was also responsible for the Ramsbottom UDC fleet.) On 1 April 1968 the Haslingden and Rawtenstall fleets were finally joined together to form the Rossendale Joint Transport Committee, to which Hasinglden contributed 15 buses in their pale blue and cream livery, which was soon subsumed by Rawtenstall red.

During the 1960's Todmorden JOC withdrew the Todmorden to Burnley service that Rawtenstall had been operating jointly since the early 1920's. Rawtenstall Corporation was called upon to provide replacement services between Bacup and Sharneyford, and Bacup and Burnley (jointly with Ribble Motor Services).

Rawtenstall contributed 45 vehicles when Rossendale Transport was formed with Haslingden in 1968.

6

North-East England

From Tyne to Tees

The title of most northerly municipal bus undertaking in England went to **Newcastle upon Tyne** City Transport. It was also at (or very near) the top in one other respect – financial probity.

During its entire 68-year existence, the undertaking did not claim a penny in subsidy from the corporation, something that fewer and fewer other departments could make by the 1960's. During the good years the department ploughed substantial sums into the council coffers and it ended its existence with substantial reserves. This had been achieved despite wages for department staff increasing by four times the rate of fares during this period.

It is little wonder, therefore, that in a farewell valedictory in 1969, the then chairman of the transport committee (and later Conservative MP), Neville Trotter, welcomed the formation of the Tyneside Passenger Transport Authority but questioned the sense behind forming an entirely new body – the Tyneside PTE – to run buses in the city when Newcastle Corporation had proved, over many years, that it was more than capable of doing so.

Newcastle was a long time tramway stronghold – in fact, with the exception of Glasgow, it boasted the most extensive track mileage of any system in Great Britain north of Leeds.

The first motorbus services were introduced in 1912, when double-deckers were used to provide links from various tramway termini to mining villages outside the municipal boundary; these included Westerhope and Fenham although one service went as far as the upper Tyne market down of Hexham, more than 30 miles away. The first bus service originating in the city centre (to Ponteland) did not start until 1921.

A change of policy was initiated following a 1929 agreement with LNER, by which Newcastle Transport withdrew from several of its 'beyond boundary' services, in return for railway company buses not competing with the corporation on the busy and lucrative West Road.

This situation was compounded in 1936 when the corporation transferred its services to Cramlington and Seaton Sluice to United Automobile Services in return for the latter's interest in services to Ponteland and Darras Hall, to be followed two years later with the Stockfield service also going over to United. By 1938 the corporation operated 14 motorbus routes.

Perhaps Newcastle's diminished interest in country services was due to the trolleybus developments taking place within the city proper. The first route – a crosstown, east-west service from Denton Square to Wallsend, was introduced in October 1935. It was an immediate success and a rapid expansion of trolleybus wiring followed, even in some instances replacing motorbuses that had been experimented with on new routes to peripheral housing estates. Expansion of the trolley

THE CORPORATION BUS

network resumed after world war and although consolidation was the name of the game during most of the 1950's, a new wiring arrangement brought the route mileage to a record 37 miles in 1958.

To most observers, the future of the trolleybuses must have seemed assured, especially given the fuel rationing brought about by the Suez crisis just two years earlier. Then, in 1962, the corporation did a complete *volte face* and announced its intention to run down the trolleybus system. The programme of abandonment began the following year and by October 1966 one of the largest networks in the country had gone – the pioneering Denton Square to Wallsend service being the last.

After just three years of all-motorbus operation Newcastle City Transport itself passed into history. Just before closure the undertaking was operating 134 route miles over 58 services, most of them terminating within a four-mile radius of the city centre, although there were still a few out of town routes, e.g. to Throckley – an expanding village to the west, and to Tynemouth in the east where the river of the same name meets the North Sea.

One distinguishing feature of the Newcastle undertaking was colour scheming. Corporation trams were painted in maroon but buses, when they began in earnest, were painted blue (a very dark blue), and in fact were marketed as 'Blue Bus Services'. But when trolleybuses were introduced they appeared in yellow and in 1949 – with the tram system in its final year – it became corporation policy for all buses to wear this colour.

However, this did not stop older Geordies retaining a habit of referring to corporation buses as "blue buses", apparently for many years after the changeover to yellow had taken place.

Located diagonally from Newcastle on the south bank of the River Tyne, **South Shields** was, in *pro rata* terms, an even bigger operator of trolleybuses – with more trolleys than motorbuses in the fleet until the last two years before closure in 1964.

Despite this the first corporation buses were motorbuses, albeit of the petrol-electric variety; these were introduced in 1914 – operating a service between the Stanhope Road tram terminus and Simonside - and were replaced by petrol engine vehicles five years later.

Despite being a relatively latecomer to electric tramway operation (in 1906), South Shields Corporation set up an intensive network in a figure of eight, which was laid in accordance of the shape of the town and ensured that no citizen was any more than one quarter of a mile's walk of a tram stop. As a result the motorbus fleet remained small – indeed it had grown to only ten vehicles by 1934 - and when it was decided to abandon the trams, in 1936, trolleybuses were the council's preferred option.

Twelve trolleybus routes were planned to replace the trams. These stuck to the tram route 'core' but, being more flexible, were able to be fanned out to serve a wider variety of terminal points. A milestone was reached in 1938 when the wires were extended along the Coast Road to Marsden Bay and, a year later, to the popular local attraction, Marsden Grotto.

After world war two, trolleybuses replaced the last tram route along King George Road to the Ridgeway, there was a new route to The Lawe, and a second service to Horsley Hill Estate. Then, as in several other locations where trolleybus numbers were higher, or on a par with, their motorbus counterparts, expansion of the former just stopped dead.

There then followed an eight-year period of consolidation until the first major contraction in 1958 when the service to Marsden Grotto was discontinued. However, the mystery is that it survived so long, given that much of the demand was seasonal; the headway was just 30 minutes (totally uneconomic for trolleybuses) and the wires were subject to corrosion from salt coming off the North Sea.

With trolleybuses still playing a major role in moving people around, it took six years for the system to be wound down; by the last year the overhead was in a particularly bad state and dewirements were common, even on long straight stretches. The end came on 19 April 1964 and, remarkably, there was no closure ceremony – in contrast to the scene on 12 October 1936 when a large crowd flocked to the Market Place to see the first service trolleybus set off.

For most of the existence of the South Shields tramway, livery was maroon and cream and several experiments were used on motorbuses. However, when the then new trolleybuses were delivered coloured blue with yellow relief, this became the livery for motorbuses and trams as well.

The hub of the system, in both the trolleybus era and thereafter, was the Market Place, which on destination screens was truncated to 'Market'. At its peak, the fleet size stood at just over 100 vehicles. Branding was succinct but effective – the lower panels carrying 'South Shields' without any reference to corporation or county borough, with the coat of arms centred below.

The undertaking was absorbed by Tyneside PTE in January 1970 and soon South Shields buses were painted in the yellow of the dominant partner, Newcastle. For a while, a blue strip was used to distinguish the South Shields part of the new operation although what this meant to locals – if anything at all – is not clear.

The corporation bus had something of an unusual arrival in **Sunderland**, because the local authority launched its first two routes without actually owning any vehicles or employing any crews.

Thus when Sunderland Corporation began a service in February 1928, it did so with hired vehicles and platform staff from the Northern General Transport Company, an arrangement that was extended in May of that year when a second route was launched.

The first corporation-owned buses did not arrive in the town until the next year when, coincidentally, Sunderland launched its third route in a joint agreement with Northern General. By the outbreak of world war two in 1939, the system had expanded to ten routes, many of them launched to serve the housing estates that had grown up on the then periphery of the town.

There was just one tram extension after 1945 and further expansion of the transport system was given over to buses, as a result of which the fleet expanded rapidly. The early post war years were a boom period for passenger usage, although the undertaking must have been adversely affected by the deaths, in service, of two general managers in fairly quick succession, one in 1948 and then again in 1952. This paved the way for the arrival of Norman Morton who was to remain in charge until the final year of the department's existence, when he left in controversial circumstances.

Within months of Mr Morton's arrival, three major decisions had been taken – a plan for the abandonment of the remaining tramway services, the introduction of

THE CORPORATION BUS

service numbers for buses and a change in the livery from red and cream to green and cream.

The first numbering scheme showed 14 services, numbered from 1 to 11 and then 13, 15 and 18. Six of these services terminated in the central area, the destination screen for inward journeys carrying the somewhat unspecific 'Town'. Short workings on each service, even where there was more than one, were marked with the suffix, X.

Another achievement by Mr Morton was to reach an accord with Northern General, with whom Sunderland Corporation had been increasingly at odds (ironic given their earlier mutuality) over new routes to the ever-expanding peripheral housing estates.

By 1960, which marked the diamond jubilee of municipal transport in Sunderland, the bus fleet numbered around 200 vehicles operating 25 services, which were: 1, Town-Grangetown; 2 and 3, Town-Farringdon; 4, Vilette Road-Red House South; 5, Vilette Road-Red House North; 6, Grangetown-Southwick; 7, Town-Prestbury Road; 8, Seaburn Camp-Leechmere Road; 9, Helmsdale Road-Docks; 10, Grangetown-Pennywell; 11, Town-Ford Estate; 11, Town-Front Road; 12, Fullwell-Humbledon; 13, Red House-Humbledon; 14, Fullwell-Humbledon; 15, Docks-Telford Road; 16, Town-Grindon; 17, Town-Hylton Castle; 18, Seaburn Camp-Springwell; 19, Town-Seaburn circle (via Park Avenue); 20, Town-Seaburn circle (via Sea Front); 21, Tunstall Road-Dean Estate (via Newcastle Road); 22, Tunstall Road-Dean Estate (via Fulwell Road); 23, Thornley Close-Ambleside Terrace; 24, Seaburn Camp-Durham Road; 48, Sunderland-North Hylton (joint service with Northern General sporting same number).

A watershed arrived in 1966 when a flat fare was introduced throughout the system. This cost four old pence, and there were discounts for tokens purchased in batches of ten. Always controversial, the method of fare collection was rescinded in 1970 by order of the transport committee, a move which Mr Morton felt gave him no alternative to resign (although there were other issues which also put him at odds with some local politicians).

By this time it was already known that Sunderland Corporation would be absorbed within the new Tyneside Passenger Transport Executive in April 1973 but with morale at a low ebb the corporation eventually decided to hand over the assets of the undertaking to the PTE a year before it was strictly necessary – in contrast to most other local authorities in the metropolitan areas who seemed to want to hang on to their own distinctive buses until the very last moment.

Although the name might suggest otherwise, **West Hartlepool** is by far the bigger of the two Hartlepools (the other is simply 'Hartlepool'). This was reflected in the size of the respective corporation bus fleets at the dawn of the 1960's when the West Hartlepool fleet numbered around 60 and Hartlepool just four.

West Hartlepool inaugurated its first regular motorbus service on 4 April 1921, jointly with Middlesbrough Corporation, between Seaton Carew and Port Clarence, via the Tees Transporter Bridge.

In 1923, the Foggy Furze trams ceased running and this was temporarily replaced by motorbuses until trolleybuses took over the following year. By 1927, all remaining tram services had been replaced by trolleybuses.

Soon after the end of world war two, the corporation announced that motorbuses would take over the trolleybus services; Seaton Carew was the first route to be converted and the final trolleybus service – a joint working with Hartlepool – closed in 1953.

Conversion to one-man operation (and to a complete single deck fleet) began in 1964, although this had still to be achieved by 1968 when the two Hartlepools merged to form a single authority – and single municipal transport undertaking.

Just six years later this undertaking too came to an end when it was joined to the new local authority of Cleveland, which operated under the American-style banner of 'Cleveland Transit'.

At one time **Hartlepool** had the distinction of operating the smallest fleet of corporation buses in England.

However, this was an improvement on the situation in 1953, when Hartlepool arranged to begin a joint route with West Hartlepool which required each to provide half of the buses to operate the service and at the time the number of buses owned by Hartlepool at the time was precisely nil.

Initially negotiations with United Counties reached an advanced stage but the agreement reached was eventually with Bee Line Roadways, a local coach operator, who ran the service on Hartlepool Corporation's behalf from 1 August.

The Hartlepool Corporation 'bus fleet', consisting of four ex-London Transport Bristols liveried in blue and cream, was garaged at the Bee Line depot in York Road, West Hartlepool, with any vehicle shortages being met from Bee Line's own fleet.

The anomaly ended on 1 April 1967 when the two Hartlepools, and their respective bus fleets, were merged.

Sunderland and the two Hartlepools were all located on the coast; further south and inland lay **Stockton on Tees,** on the north bank of the River Tees, across from which lay Yorkshire.

Until 1921, tramways on Teesside were operated by the Imperial chemical company but in 1921 the system was divided among three local municipalities – Stockton, Middlesbrough and Thornaby on Tees.

Thornaby relinquished its interest before the trams closed down but Stockton launched its first buses to coincide with the tramway takeover within its boundaries and gradually built up a thriving undertaking that throughout its existence was rarely a drain on the rates.

For the first 25 years of the undertaking's history, livery was the same as the trams – red and cream. However, in 1947 this was changed to green and cream and coincided with the shunning of external advertising, a move probably not unconnected with a similar strategy some years earlier at neighbouring Middlesbrough.

The absence of advertising made it possible for maintenance employees to decorate one bus every Christmas time with an animated, illuminated display involving a 'moving' reindeer and Santa. Apparently the display would not have shamed one of Blackpool's illuminated trams and children marvelled whenever the decorated vehicle appeared on the streets.

Among the Stockton services were two operated jointly with Middlesbrough and because the latter used letters rather than numbers for service identification, one was branded the letter 'O' (in Middlesbrough style) and the other the number '11' (in Stockton style). Other services extended beyond the boundary to Billingham and Thornaby.

THE CORPORATION BUS

In 1968, the creation of the new borough of Teesside saw the Stockton and Middlesbrough undertakings merge, with the two donating around 90 vehicles each. The new organisation was called Teesside Municipal Transport, which, with appropriate political astuteness, carried a livery of turquoise – a mixture of Stockton green and Middlesbrough blue. As amalgamation loomed, Stockton placed some new deliveries in service sporting the new colour – but still proudly wearing Stockton fleet-names.

At the start of the 1960's County Durham boasted six municipal undertakings, making it third in the county pecking order after Lancashire and Yorkshire. From a historical perspective the sixth of these, **Darlington,** is best known for the railway link to Stockton, opened in 1825, but in bus terms the demise of the corporation undertaking was probably the saddest of all the municipal operators post-privatisation.

Staying true to coal-fired electric traction, Darlington Corporation opted for an all-trolleybus system to replace the tram fleet in 1926. All the vehicles were initially single deck and double-deckers did not appear on the streets of the town until 1949. At its peak the (all trolleybus) fleet strength was 95 vehicles and for many years Darlington town centre hummed with the gentle sound of trolleybuses, with various wiring permutations stretching right around the Market Place and town hall.

The first corporation motorbus did not make an appearance until 1950 and despite the town's proximity to the Durham coalfield, a decision to replace the trolleys with diesels was made the following year, although the programme was not completed until 1957 with the number 3 service from Faverdale to Neasham Road being the last to be operated under the wires.

However, the undertaking remained attached to single-deckers and in the early 1960's these still constituted around 40 per cent of the total fleet – the biggest proportion in any municipal undertaking outside the very smallest in north and south Wales.

The livery was dark blue and cream but, as happened elsewhere, cream gradually became the dominant colour with blue relegated to a relief role. After 1974 the new district council stuck with the coat of arms but on deregulation in 1986 the new arm's length company was registered as Darlington Transport Co and branded under DTC.

Catchy though the new abbreviated title may have been, it did not protect what had been a small but efficient municipal operation from the cold winds of competition. By the summer of 1994 the situation had deteriorated to the extent that the council offered the bus company for sale and eventually bids were received from Badgerline (predecessor of First), Stagecoach and, the preferred bidder, Yorkshire Traction. Outbid by YT, Stagecoach launched what became known as a 'bus war', which depleted the number of DTC staff and, with it the level of service.

Consequently, the other bidders withdrew their offer and the saga ended with the duty supervisor at DTC one afternoon calling all drivers to return to the depot once their vehicles had reached their respective termini. The date was 11 November – but it was surrender rather than an armistice.

7

Yorkshire and Lincolnshire

Bus Ridings

As any proud Yorkshireman is never slow in telling you, 'God's own county' became so big it had to be split into three sub-sections – the North, West and East Ridings.

The North Riding is largely rural so not surprisingly, if the corporation bus was to be found anywhere there it had to be in overwhelmingly industrial **Middlesbrough**, which although located on the south side of the River Tees, and in Yorkshire, is commonly mistaken to be in County Durham.

Middlesbrough was another late starter in terms of municipal transport, local tramways having been operated up to 1921 by the Imperial chemical company. Corporation buses were introduced at the same time as the tramway was taken over by the local authority. Operation commenced in April with 31 tramcars and five motorbuses acquired, with the corporation's share of the Imperial Tramways undertaking, augmented by six new motor buses bought in readiness. Buses ran from the Exchange in the town centre to Grove Hill and to

Stokesley and from Port Clarence (Transporter Bridge) to Seaton Carew (joint with West Hartlepool Corporation) and to Haverton Hill.

Shortly after the last tram service closed, a new manager arrived in the form of Frank Lythgoe, who was previously at Rawtenstall. By all accounts he was a remarkably clever fellow who turned Middlesbrough from a mediocre operation into one that became a template for cleanliness and operating efficiency.

By the time of Mr Lythgoe's appointment, Middlesbrough had adopted letters rather than numbers for route identification, although one exception was the 11, operated jointly with neighbouring Stockton.

Passenger numbers soared after world war two and 1949 saw the launch of services I to Saltersgill, L (Link) from West Lane via Ladgate Lane to Brambles Farm, T to Tollesby and Y to Thorntree (Greenway). In 1952 services E and F were separated, and in 1953 the Q and R circular replaced the I service. Service N commenced to Berwick Hills in 1953 and was extended in 1955. Service U to Park End was introduced in 1954, and the Z to Park End via Marton Road in 1957, in which year the Billingham 11 was extended to Rievaulx Avenue. The U and Z operated as a circular from 1960, though without through fares across the outer terminus. The B was extended to Stainton in 1961 and the Z diverted to Easterside from 1963. Some journeys on service O were diverted to Blue Hall at Norton in 1965, but reverted to Norton Green in 1966.

Middlesbrough livery was dark blue and the buses always looked very smart, even though relief colouring (in this case cream) was kept to a minimum. As part of his policy, Mr Lythgoe ordered that the undertaking should refuse to accept external advertising, arguing that smart, pristine buses were more likely to attract passengers. This policy continued beyond his retirement in 1964 and, indeed, lasted until the end of Middlesbrough Corporation Transport.

Middlesbrough also had a third share in the other local authority undertaking in the North Riding – the **Teesside Rail-less Traction Board**, which it operated in conjunction with Eston Urban District Council (who owned the remaining two thirds). This organisation boasted a trolleybus network linking North Ormsby (in Middlesbrough) with Grangetown, South Bank in Eston and which operated within one of the most gloomily industrial areas in the country, characterised by chemicals, iron, steel and shipbuilding – factors which reflected the rather sombre dark green livery of the buses. Launched in 1919, this system also became part of Teesside Municipal Transport in 1968 but closed three years later in what was Britain's penultimate trolleybus abandonment.

Despite the presence of 'rail-less' in its title, TRTB actually operated more motorbuses than trolleybuses (24 compared to 15 in the early 1960's).

Not surprisingly, the largest concentration of Yorkshire municipals was to be found in the West Riding, where the bulk of the population lay.

The seventh largest municipal operator in the country, **Leeds** was a tram stronghold for longer than most cities as the decision to fully abandon was not made until 1953, and trams carried on running until 14 November 1959 – a depressing day when the heavens opened and nature seemed to join in the mourning for what had, at its peak, been one of premier tramway systems in the country.

The corporation first ran motorbuses in 1906 and launched a trolleybus line in 1911 (just four days after Bradford's launch) between Aire Street, near City Square, through New Farnley to the city boundary. A second line, from Guisely to Bury in Wharfdale and Otley, and well outside the city limits, was launched in 1915 but there were no more extensions after that and the the last trolleybus ran in 1928. Trams remained strong for the next quarter of a century and it was not until the early 1950's that the bus became the dominant mode of transport.

Trams had been painted in dark blue up to 1948, when a change was made to an equally impressive dark red. Dark green was chosen for buses in 1950 and although colour is a subjective matter, their livery does seem, in retrospect, decidedly gloomy compared with that of the trams. However the dark green was relieved by a lighter Lincoln green above the windows of the lower deck saloon. Over the years the Lincoln green portion grew as a percentage of the overall external area and eventually become the majority colour in a two-tone livery.

Leeds had introduced motorbuses in 1913, just a year after the trolleys, and the corporation later entered into one of those joint agreement with railway-owned buses that so typified the Yorkshire scene. However, in this case the agreement fell in 1931 following a disagreement relating to the ownership of tram routes in the Leeds 'B' area.

Leeds boasted an extensive service network covering all parts of the city and some of the communities beyond the boundary. A few of the services were run jointly with Bradford Corporation and the West Riding Automobile Company. In the final year of the undertaking service numbers went from 1 to 84, with few breaks, with two more – 89 and 97 – somewhat isolated from the main sequence. Most routes were cross-town although 20 services started and ended at the Central Bus Station, which was rebuilt in 1963, the original having opened in 1938.

There were also 15 park and ride services – marketed as 'Fastway' – numbered between 222 and 231.

Leeds City Transport – to give the undertaking its official name - had a reputation for being innovative and experimentally minded and Park & Ride had been introduced as early as 1965. Motorists were given the 'stick' of restricted and more expensive car parking in the city centre and P&R was supposed to be the 'carrot' but it was a total disaster, attracting just 115 passengers in the first ten days of operation. This was despite a bus every ten minutes during the two hours of the morning rush hour and one hour and 40 minutes in the evening.

Nevertheless the department persevered and when Fastway was introduced in 1967 patronage was infinitely greater than what went before.

Leeds' penchant for innovation plus a "special partnership" with the Ministry of Transport, led to the inauguration of a special city centre shuttle service, linking the main railway station, bus station and the prime shopping area, much of which had been pedestrianised.

After complaints about shoppers being subjected to diesel fumes in a pedestrian location, in 1972 the department took part in a government-sponsored experiment using a battery-operated minibus for the city centre shuttle. After three months in Leeds the bus was sent first to Sheffield and then to Birmingham but the experiment never led to this type of vehicle being used in any great numbers – either in Leeds or elsewhere. Meanwhile, complaints about fumes from the diesel minibuses continued, as did objections to the very principle of allowing buses on a pedestrian precinct; as a result the shuttle service was rerouted from September 1972 so that it used only *bona fide* roads.

Leeds City Transport was proud of its ability to 'think outside the box' (as we would say nowadays) and for this reason local politicians strongly opposed the takeover of the undertaking by West Yorkshire PTE, on the basis that all the desired improvements in public transport could be achieved by the bus services remaining in local municipal control. But this view held little sway at either Westminster or Whitehall and the rest, as they say, is history.

THE CORPORATION BUS

1. Salford City Transport buses at Victoria Bus Station. In the background is Manchester Exchange railway station – actually in Salford. *North-east Bus Photos*

2. This picture is probably pre-1955, when Birkenhead switched the fleetname from Corporation Transport to Municipal Transport. *North-east Bus Photos*

YORKSHIRE AND LINCOLNSHIRE

3. A handsome double-decker of Southampton Corporation on duty in the city's famous Common. *North-east Bus Photos*

4. This Reading Corporation trolleybus is on the flagship Wokingham Road-Tilehurst route. *North-east Bus Photos*

THE CORPORATION BUS

5. Hull Corporation's bold streamline livery in blue and white lasted well into the 1960's, by which time the form of design had been abandoned by most other municipal operators. *North-east Bus Photos*

6. Blackpool Corporation persisted with full-cab frontages long after it had abandoned centre doors in favour of open rear entrances. *North-east Bus Photos*

YORKSHIRE AND LINCOLNSHIRE

7. Rear and front engine corporation buses on duty in the centre of Coventry in the 1960's, when cream began to overtake red as the primary colour. *North-east Bus Photos*

8. Like many smaller operators Lytham St Annes Corporation boasted a striking colour scheme, in this case blue with white relief. *North-east Bus Photos*

THE CORPORATION BUS

9. Service number 5X signifies a short working in Sunderland. To the casual observer almost every Sunderland Corporation bus seemed to carry external advertising for the Binns department store. *North East Bus Photos*

10. Municipal pride on Tayside. Such large script fell out of favour after world war two when operators gradually began to use advertising on upper panels to help alleviate rising costs. *Author*

YORKSHIRE AND LINCOLNSHIRE

11. An early double-decker operated by Glasgow Corporation. This vehicle can be seen today at the Scottish Vintage Bus Museum. *Author*

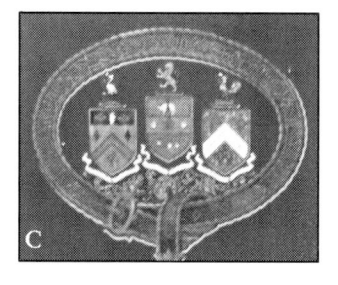

12. The municipal coat of arms was the key part of corporation bus branding, in this case South Shields (A), Aberdeen (B) and Burnley, Colne & Nelson (C). *Author*

THE CORPORATION BUS

13. Chester was an early user of sliding doors as an addition to passenger comfort. *Author*

14. Middlesbrough was one of a few undertakings that shunned external advertising until the very end of their existence. *Author*

YORKSHIRE AND LINCOLNSHIRE

15. Corporation buses no longer ply the Prom at Morecambe – but at least Typhoo Tea is still with us. *Author*

16. Buses from a variety of municipal operators (like Rochdale, pictured) could be seen at various terminal points in Manchester city centre. This is Cannon Street bus station. *North-east Bus Photos*

THE CORPORATION BUS

Bradford was one of the most chronicled of all the corporation bus undertakings, principally because it was the first and last to operate trolleybuses in the UK and for many years boasted the most extensive municipal trolleybus mileage (which effectively made it the biggest outside London).

Indeed, the trolleybus preceded the motorbus in Bradford by 15 years, the former being launched in June 1911 with a service between Laisterdyke and Dudley Hill. Motorbuses did not put in an appearance until 1926, the first scheduled service operating from Lister Park to Bankfoot.

From then on both motorbus and trolleybus services grew in tandem, causing the previously large tramway system to go into decline, eventually closing in 1950.

The following year, came the highly significant appointment, as manager, of the wonderfully-named Chaceley T Humpidge, who had previously served in the same capacity at Rochdale. Mr Humpdige was a strong supporter of the trolley vehicle and for the next ten years the Bradford system experienced a long Indian summer under his guidance, with trolleybuses actually replacing several motorbus services in a complete reversal of the situation in most other locations.

At its peak, in early 1962, the trolleybus system covered 47 route miles and was worked by around 200 vehicles. Both trolley and motorbuses sported a pleasant light blue livery with some cream relief.

For many years the Bradford fleet stood at a roughly equal number of motorbuses and trolleybuses. Fluctuations in the price of oil and coal caused the economic situation to see-saw; sometimes these favoured the motorbus, at other times the trolleybus.

However, with the departure of Mr Humpidge to manage Sheffield City Transport in 1961, out went the impetus for further trolleybus expansion although even had he remained it is difficult to see how this could have been achieved to any great extent, given that the trolleybus was about to fall from grace in those cities and towns where it still operated in substantial numbers. Nevertheless, although the succeeding manager, Edward Deakin, recommended abandonment he did not believe in taking out vehicles with many years of serviceable life just to be rid of them. The abandonment scheme that followed was structured and methodical and the department showed itself at being very adept at constructing temporary or replacement wiring while the central area was undergoing massive redevelopment.

The first stage in the withdrawal of the trolleybuses came with the closure of the City to Bradford Moor, and the Eccleshill to St. Enoch's Road services in November 1962 and another nine years elapsed before trolleybuses left the streets of Bradford for the last time, after giving more than 60 years of service to the city.

By the time of the last trolleybus, one-man operation had been permitted on double deck diesels for six years but Bradford was reluctant to adopt the process, apparently because the traffic manager at the time took a view that the so-called benefits were overrated. He believed that the obvious financial and crew roster advantages were negated by the fact that rear-engine buses were less reliable than their front engine predecessors and the extra time needed for the drivers to collect fares led to longer journeys and, consequently, further passenger disillusionment. He also considered it a mistake to break up duos of drivers and conductors who had worked together for many years and developed as a 'team', to the advantage of the travelling public.

Later a national study concluded that, when everything was taken into account, one-man, as opposed to two-man, operation of buses produced an average cost saving of 13 per cent for each undertaking – substantial but not enormous. Perhaps the man at Bradford had a point and things were less clear-cut than they seemed.

For the greater part of its existence, the corporation bus scene in **Huddersfield** was also characterised by trolleybuses. To the stranger, this was evident as soon as he or she alighted from the railway station, where huge six-wheeler trolleybuses queued for passengers or could be seen terminating at the large turning oval on St George's Square.

There were also extensive cross-town services to which trolleybus operation was distinctly suited in this hilly location. Huddersfield may not have boasted the largest trolleybus network in Britain, but on a *pro rata* basis of trolleybuses related to overall bus mileage, size and population, it was at or near the top of the league. Just before the programme of trolleybus abandonment began in earnest, the electric vehicles accounted for more than half of the Huddersfield fleet of more than 200 buses.

Powers to operate motorbus services had been acquired in 1913 but the first service did not commence until seven years later and even this was a shuttle, with journeys to and from the town centre having to be made by tramcar. The first 'end to end' service by motorbus was launched in 1924. The first interurban service (with Halifax) began the following year.

However many of the later tram conversions were by trolleybus and such was the influence of this mode of transport that when the first route was abandoned, that to West Vale in 1961, it was replaced by the first motorbus service introduced solely by Huddersfield Corporation since 1930.

Here was another joint omnibus operating area that the corporation shared with British Rail bus services, and it lasted much longer than in Leeds. The replacement of further trolley services in 1966 (Brackenhill-Lockwood; Riddings-Newsome South) was used to exercise a co-ordination with several JOC services

The decision to abandon the entire trolleybus network - in the face of severe local opposition - had been taken in 1962 but it was not until 1968 that the final service, from Birkby to Crosland Hill, came to an end.

Following the formation of the National Bus Company in 1969, the JOC agreement came to an end in October of that year, with the corporation taking over all the previously worked joint services.

Huddersfield livery was what has been described as 'Post Office red' with cream relief. The lower panels of the buses carried 'Huddersfield' in large script, although on some vehicles the coat of arms appeared at the centre of the lower front, but all branding versions reflected the local and municipal pride that the fleet engendered. This was lost in 1974 when not only Huddersfield Corporation Transport disappeared (to

THE CORPORATION BUS

become part of West Yorkshire PTE) but the very name Huddersfield itself was extinguished from the administrative map as a result of becoming part of the extended Kirklees District Council within the new West Yorkshire Metropolitan County. Ah well, at least Huddersfield Town FC did not change its name to 'Kirklees United' or something similarly dreadful (as if the fans would have allowed it anyway).

The corporation bus made its debut in **Halifax** in October 1912 on a service from the Rook Hotel on Queen's Road to Mount Tabor, this later being extended to Wainstalls. A second service, from Alexandra Street to Siddal, was launched on January the following year.

There was a brief flirtation with trolleybuses between 1921 and 1924 when three vehicles were operated, including the two that had provided Scotland's pioneer service in Dundee just before world war one.

In 1929 Halifax secured trial use of a new type of AEC double-decker, after an earlier trial had been carried out in Glasgow, with the vehicle finished in that city's (then unique) livery of green, orange and cream. The transport committee was extremely impressed by the performance of the vehicle, particularly on the hilly terrain that characterised the town and its surroundings. But they were also highly taken with colour scheme and green, orange and cream soon replaced red and cream (which itself had superseded blue and cream) as the standard Halifax livery.

Meanwhile, the Transport Act of 1928 had paved the way for a Halifax Joint Omnibus Committee, consisting of four representatives from the corporation and railway-owned buses. The revenue from all services entirely within the borough (classed as 'A' services) went to the corporation, all revenue from services that did not enter the borough (classed as 'B' services) went to the JOC, while revenue from JOC services that did enter the borough was apportioned between the corporation and the JOC. Also, other operators made compensatory payments to Halifax Corporation representing passenger fares taken within the borough. A third category (classed as 'C' services) were the longer distance routes operating beyond the 'B' category area that were operated by the railway companies (or their nominees).

Later, Halifax became something of a pioneer in terms of comfort and safety; every bus built for the corporation since 1956 came with a front-entrance, automatic door, and by the diamond jubilee of the undertaking, on April 1968, only 23 buses with open platforms remained in use.

At the jubilee, the integrated Corporation/JOC services, boasted a total of 182 buses, 94 of which belonged to Halifax Corporation and many of these were single-deckers, equipped for one-man operation. The corporation operated 20 core services, numbered between 1 and 36, some operating cross-town and others terminating in the central area. However beyond-boundary services accounted for a substantial majority of the 175 route miles of the JOC area.

Showing that size did not preclude municipal transport, the small town of **Todmorden,** on the edge of the Pennines, launched its own bus system in 1907, operating local routes but extending this to several destinations elsewhere in Yorkshire and in Lancashire.

THE CORPORATION BUS

In 1929 Todmorden became the fourth Yorkshire undertaking to enter into a joint services agreement with local bus operations owned by the railway companies and the vehicles carried the municipal coat of arms and the LMS, and latterly British Rail, crests.

Remarkably Todmorden lasted until 1971 when its 12-strong fleet of green and cream buses was absorbed into the Calderdale Joint Omnibus Committee, which also included BR and the Halifax JOC (but not Halifax Corporation).

In stark contrast was **Sheffield**, the largest municipal operator in Yorkshire (and fifth largest in the country). With its hilly terrain and concentrated population of more than half a million, the city would have seemed an ideal location for a large and intensive trolleybus network. However Sheffield was one of two large English undertakings to eschew trolleybuses.

The main reason was Sheffield's loyalty to the tram; this remained the premier form of local transport until after world war two and the decision to abandon the system was not taken until 1951. The last service closed in October, 1960, bringing traditional tramway operation in England (with the unique exception of Blackpool) to an end.

An extensive tramway system had been built up by 1913, the year that the first buses, which were double-deckers, arrived in the city, mainly on tramway feeder services. The first tramway conversion, in 1935, involved a relatively short route but from then on buses gradually became the mainstay of transport for those new housing estates that pushed the city outward (and in the particular case of Sheffield, upward).

Up to that period the primary bus livery had been dark blue with cream relief but then a decision was made in council to make cream the dominant colour, principally to relieve the sooty image of this most industrial of major cities. Inevitably, this policy meant increased costs for washing and cleaning but to its credit the transport department was up to the task and for many years Sheffield was famous in transport circles for having "spotless" buses in a city that certainly wasn't!

Another welcome consequence of the change of livery was the opportunities it provided for experimentation with the relief colour, which was the same dark blue that had been replaced by cream. Thus sometimes blue replaced cream on the roofs; on some buses there might be a distinctive blue band separating the upper and lower decks; on others the blue might be restricted to the window panels. The result was a great deal of variety within a large fleet, which nevertheless managed to retain a basic corporate identity.

By the time the last tram ran in 1960, Sheffield boasted approximately 700 vehicles. However added to this could be more than 200 other buses which belonged to Sheffield Corporation's partners in one of those joint omnibus committee agreements, already mentioned, with the railway companies (later British Railways). The operations of the committee, which was formed in 1929, took the same form as elsewhere, namely there was an A section for city services, B for intermediate services beyond the city boundary and C for longer distance routes. Although the C services and vehicles belonged entirely to the railways and those in the B category were shared between the railway and the corporation, all the vehicles carried Sheffield livery and fleet name (although only 'city' buses carried the coat of

THE CORPORATION BUS

arms). The area of the JOC was extensive, and a 'Sheffield' bus could be spotted as far away as Manchester, more than 40 miles distant.

As a result of this 'Sheffield' (in its various forms) operated a substantial number of services. After the end of the trams, bus service numbers extended from 1 to 99 with very few interruptions then another 12 in the '100' series. There were three bus stations in the city centre – Bridge, Street, Castle Street and Central or Pond Street (opposite Midland railway station), where around 30 services, both 'local' and long distance, terminated.

In 1974 this was swept away with the formation of South Yorkshire PTE, which merged the Sheffield transport department with those of Rotherham and Doncaster. This coincided with the formation of South Yorkshire Metropolitan County, although most locals no doubt still considered themselves part of the historic West Riding.

Rotherham was Yorkshire's third trolleybus pioneer, opening a line as early as October 1912 from the tram terminus at the Stag Inn at Heppingthorpe Lane to Maltby via Bramley and Wickersley.

The corporation was also quick off the mark on the motorbus front too, introducing three services in 1913, although the outbreak of world war one curtailed further expansion in the short to medium term.

Trolleybus wires were extended into Rotherham town centre in 1923 and an agreement with the private Mexborough & Swinton company permitted corporation trolleys to run as far as Conisburgh on the wires of the former. Meanwhile, motorbus expansion resumed, largely by buying out local private operators; this led to a joint service between the towns by Rotherham and Doncaster corporations.

By 1934 there was only one tram service left in operation – the long route to Templeborough, where Rotherham and Sheffield cars met at the boundary of the two boroughs. Rotherham wanted to turn this service over to trolleybus operation but Sheffield demurred and this last tramcar service operated by Rotherham Corporation survived until 1946.

Like Mexborough & Swinton, the Rotherham trolleybuses were single-deck and their limited capacity was becoming a financial disadvantage at a time when costs began to rise. This led to several service abandonments (including the pioneer route to Wickersley) or cutbacks and for a while it looked as if the entire system was earmarked for closure. This, however, would have involved the corporation in huge capital expenditure on replacement diesel buses and with the trolleys basically having plenty of life left in them, it was decided to re-body most of the fleet as double-deckers, although six single-deckers remained. Thus in one stroke the management was able to increase capacity and alleviate staff shortages, which had become a growing problem.

This, essentially, gave Rotherham trolleybuses a ten-year stay of execution and the end did not come until October 1965, with the closure of the cross-town route between Kimberworth and Thryberg.

Rotherham livery, since 1919, had been blue and white and in April 1974 this was mixed in with Sheffield cream and Doncaster red as each of the three undertakings became the property of the South

THE CORPORATION BUS

Yorkshire PTE – later branded, somewhat patronisingly, as "South Yorkshire's Transport".

The first **Doncaster** Corporation motorbus ran in 1922 but during the period up to world war two the town showed a preference for trolleybuses to be used for tram replacement services

However with peacetime the development of new routes was motorbus-orientated. A through route between Clay Lane and Sandford Road was introduced and the service to Sheffield was re-routed to allow the use of double-deck vehicles.

In 1956 the Bentley trolleybus service was converted to motorbus operation, due to a bridge replacement scheme on part of the route. Being located in the heart of the South Yorkshire coalfield, it might have been thought that, politically at least, Doncaster trolleybuses were among the safest in the country yet in 1961 the decision to eventually abandon them was announced, mainly, it seemed, because of large-scale road reconstruction in the town centre. Trolleybuses then comprised around a quarter of total fleet strength.

Closure was planned for four or five years in the future but took only two. In December that year trolleybus operation on the Hyde Park route ceased and in 1962 the Hexthorpe, Balby and Wheatley Hills routes were abandoned, leaving only the Racecourse and Beckett Road routes, which were abandoned, respectively, in October and December 1963.

As was the case elsewhere, Doncaster introduced one-man operation on single-deck vehicles in the early 1960's, including on the ex-trolleybus routes to Hyde

Park, Hexthorpe and the Racecourse, with double-deck operation following in the 1970's.

A new route to West Bessacar was introduced in April 1973 and in December of the same year a circular route around the town commenced, using, in both cases, new Seddon midi-buses.

The only municipal operator in the East Riding, **Hull** boasted arguably the most dramatic livery of all – a streamlined fusion of cream and mid blue.

The first corporation motorbuses had sported maroon and cream, the same livery as the trams. Open top double-deckers, they first appeared on the streets in 1909 but were withdrawn three years later and the next motorbus was not delivered until 1921. But progress was rapid after that and the fleet numbered 55 at the end of the decade, this figure doubling by 1935.

The streamlined livery was introduced in 1936 and the first trolleybus appeared the following year.

Another important development during the 1930's was a joint services agreement with East Yorkshire Motor Services, which divided the greater Hull area into three sections – A (inner), B (suburban) and B (outer). Revenue from A went wholly to the corporation, C to East Yorkshire and B was shared. This agreement lasted for almost 50 years, ending in 1981, although the A and B areas had been merged into one in 1969.

Serving the densely populated inner city districts, the trolleybuses were very profitable for the first decade after world war two but their value declined as the population spread out and the wires did not follow

THE CORPORATION BUS

them – partly due to the capital costs involved and partly due to restrictions posed by the EYMS agreement. The size of the electric fleet peaked in 1953 and after the idea was mooted in 1959, a decision to abandon the system was taken two years later.

The seven trolleybus services were closed between July 1961 and January 1964, with some of the vehicles less than ten years old.

Passenger numbers peaked (at 102 million) in 1949 and, in common with many other undertakings around this period, external advertising was allowed for the first time in 1951.

By the mid fifties, the corporation was operating 36 regular services although these were numbered up to 95, obviously with many gaps. Despite the joint services agreement, most of the corporation routes operated within the city boundary. In 1963, a major revision of service numbers took place, one of the results being that short workings of main routes were allocated the prefix "1", perhaps making the numbering system look even more complicated than before, at least to the uninitiated.

In 1961, just as the trolleybus abandonment programme was being put into operation, the fleet stood at just under 240 vehicles, just over a quarter being trolleybuses.

Back in 1949 the then manager, George Pulfrey, had engineered a striking new trolleybus, which was designed to accommodate one-man operation, although the usual opposition of the trade unions ensured this did not happen. However by the late sixties, his successor was designing a new auto-fare system with the Bell Ticket Punch company. By that time union opposition had receded and after a successful series of trials, Hull fast tracked the conversion of all its buses to one-man operation and completed the process in November 1972 – the first municipal undertaking to do so

The twin towns of Grimsby and Cleethorpes on the Lincolnshire coast pooled their passenger transport resources on 1 January 1957, to form the **Grimsby-Cleethorpes** Joint Undertaking.

However, for 20 years before that the two corporations had co-operated with a joint trolleybus service, which operated between Grimsby Market Place and the bathing pool at the southern extremity of Cleethorpes, with short working turning circles at various points in between. Grimsby had also operated a trolleybus service within the town, between Riby Square and Weelsby Road, but this was withdrawn in 1955. The trolley service between the two towns lasted until 1960.

Municipal transport operation came to Grimsby in 1925 when the corporation took over the Great Grimsby Street Tramways Company; trolleybus operation began in 1927 and motorbuses a year later. Cleethorpes UDC, which had been operating buses since 1930, purchased the local street tramways company in 1936 and a few months later became a municipal borough; abandonment of the trams soon followed.

At the start of the 1960's the joint fleet comprised around 100 vehicles. Services were numbered chronologically from 1 to 15 while there was also a joint service, number 45, to Immingham, operated with Lincolnshire Roadcar.

Grimsby's livery had been dark maroon with a little cream while that of Cleethorpes was blue and grey. The joint undertaking's vehicles were painted in dark blue and cream with the coat of arms of each town located adjacent in the lower side panels. These, however, were placed at a respectable distance in recognition of the sensibilities of the two communities who, although adjacent, in many ways were very different.

Somewhat smaller than Grimsby-Cleethorpes was Lincolnshire's only other municipal undertaking, the county town of **Lincoln** itself.

Lincoln was only slightly different from that small coterie of municipalities who ran buses but never trams. The single route of the Lincoln Tramway Company was taken over by the corporation in 1904 and electrified a year later but despite various plans, further development never materialised.

In spite of this the first buses were not placed in service until 1920. By 1927 the fleet size had grown to 27 and many parts of the city were being served; however the tramline remained in operation, partly due to height restrictions on the Roman-originated Stonebow Arch on the High Street. In December of that year Leyland demonstrated that its new low height double-decker could successfully pass through the arch; consequently, the trams were abandoned just 15 months later.

At its peak, the fleet size numbered just over 60 vehicles. Livery was a pleasant mixture of green and cream; the balance varied over the years and at one time cream was the more dominant colour. Whatever the ratio, the apple shade of green seemed most appropriate for this 'rural' city, with its magnificent cathedral dramatically situated on the top of a solitary hill set in the Lincolnshire plain.

An interesting local postscript is that shortly after deregulation, Lincoln City Transport, no doubt bowing to the changed circumstances and financial strictures, placed more than 20 taxicabs into the fleet. Whatever the benefits, this only delayed the end of municipal ownership and the council company was sold, in 1990, to its employees, who in turn sold on to Yorkshire Traction in 1993.

8

East Midlands and East Anglia

Nottingham lace and Norfolk Broads

There is much about which the city of **Nottingham** can feel proud – a fine city hall, a history of manufacturing products as diverse as lace and Raleigh bicycles, the annual Goose Fair, and two iconic football clubs – one the oldest in the Football League and the other a winner twice over of the European Cup.

Another, less well-known claim to fame, is that Nottingham was by far the largest municipal bus operator in the East Midlands and the 10th largest in the country.

Although it later also had a claim to fame related to the trolleybus, Nottingham was an early user of motorbuses, purchasing three as early as 1906 to operate a service between the city centre and the then outlying community of Carlton.

Unfortunately these vehicles proved unreliable and the motorbus did not make an appearance again until the 1920's, by which time the corporation had begun its relatively brief romance with the trolleybus.

After a visit by the transport committee to Birmingham in 1924 it was recommended to replace a single tramline route with trolleybuses, the first of which began operation in April 1927. By 1930 several more routes had been converted from tram to trolleybus including those serving Nottingham Road, Wilford Road and Wells Road, and for a brief period the fleet and system was the largest in the country.

However the most intense romances can often end abruptly and by the late 1930's Nottingham's interest in trolleybuses began to wane (towards the end of the decade the corporation had appointed a new manager, Ben England, previously at Leicester, where he had been a dedicated motorbus supporter). While other trolleybus systems underwent an 'Indian summer' in the decade after world war two, Nottingham's mostly remained static although the corporation did take over some wires abandoned by the Notts & Derby private company.

The first abandonment was small at first when services 36 and 48 were cut back slightly and, indeed, the remainder of the system remained intact for another ten years. Even after the first full service – the No 45 – to be converted to motorbus operation in November 1962, there were no further closures until April 1965. Nevertheless the bulk of the system was closed in the six months after that and the final service ran on 1 July 1966.

Meanwhile, motorbus services continued to expand and the opening of the Clifton Bridge in March 1958 had led to Clifton bus services being re-routed, a move that also heralded the start of the works services to several big name factories, including Players, Boots and Raleigh.

As one would expect in a city so strongly connected to Robin Hood, Nottingham bus livery had been mainly dark green with marginal cream relief, giving the buses a somewhat sombre appearance. In 1961, however, green was mainly restricted to the lower decks while the top deck and roofs were painted cream, although in some cases the roofs later reverted to green. The result brightened the buses considerably. After the introduction of rear-engine double-deckers in 1963, the appearance of the vehicles changed further when the front windows became curved perspect, which reduced glare for drivers but also produced a unique design which became known as the 'Nottingham look'. However one-man operation did not commence until 1970.

By the start of the 1960's, the corporation operated 53 services, numbered 1 to 59, with several breaks in the order and the undertaking owned around 430 vehicles. Buses were branded 'Nottingham City Transport' in large script above the coat of arms.

There were a number of 'beyond boundary' services, principally to West Bridgford, Carlton and Arnold. Activity beyond Nottingham was increased in 1968 when the corporation took over responsibility for the neighbouring West Bridgford Urban Council undertaking.

With the formation of West Yorkshire and South Yorkshire PTE's in 1974, Nottingham became the largest surviving municipal undertaking in England and two years later the fleet had grown to almost 500 vehicles, in contrast to the usual trends elsewhere. At the time of writing it was still the largest surviving 'municipal' in England, albeit as an arm's length council company with an 18 per cent private sector holding.

The municipal buses operated by **West Bridgford** were a symbol of that community's separate existence from its much larger neighbour, Nottingham, the centre of which was only a mile away. Even the reorganisation of local government in 1974 did not result in a Nottingham takeover, West Bridgford becoming part of a separate district called Rushcliffe.

West Bridgford was one of ten urban district councils to operate its own buses and the first in the country to do so. The first service was launched in 1914 but world war one quickly intervened, the vehicles were requisitioned and operations did not resume until after the conflict.

The first services were purely local but in 1930 the council launched a service into Nottingham, jointly with the city undertaking. However relations became less cordial in the early 1950's when Nottingham began building the Clifton Housing Estate, the only access to which was via Trent Bridge. West Bridgford opposed allowing Nottingham passage through its operating area but after a court battle the city was given the right to operate 50 per cent of services, with the remainder split equally between WBUDC and the local independent operator, South Notts.

West Bridgford was always a municipal minnow in fleet size but its dark maroon and cream buses had a reputation for being immaculately maintained and turned out. It was a pity, therefore, when in 1968 the district council felt compelled to sell the undertaking to Nottingham after failing to reach an OMO agreement, designed to reduce costs, with the trade unions

The tramway stronghold of **Leicester** first applied to operate a corporation bus service (to Thurmaston) in 1914 but this was shelved after the three vehicles delivered were requisitioned by the military following the outbreak of war in Europe.

Buses, six Tilling Stevens single-deckers, were not put into service until 1924, operating a route between

THE CORPORATION BUS

Charles Street and St Philip's Church and the first double-deckers made an appearance just a year later, providing a service between Welford Place and Southfields Place.

The early buses were intended purely as providing missing links in the tram system or as feeders to the outer tramway termini and, indeed, tramway expansion continued up to 1927, with new track laid along Coleman Road. However, as design and performance gradually improved, buses became increasingly used for more 'conventional' operations and in 1938 the manager, Ben England (shortly before his departure for Nottingham), recommended the total abandonment of the trams over a period of 15 years, although the outbreak of world war two meant the scheme had to be put on ice. By the end of hostilities, trams still accounted for 60 per cent of services operated by Leicester Corporation Transport but from 1946 the tramway conversion scheme was restarted and 160 new buses were brought into service, the last of the 11 trunk tram routes closing in 1949.

After that the bus system was extended further, principally to serve new housing estates such as New Parks, Eyres Monsell, Goodwood, Stocking Farm, Mowmacre Hill, Nether Hall, Braunstone Frith and Beaumont Leys.

One unusual feature of the Leicester undertaking was the extensive use of AEC Renown, high capacity (they boasted 66 seats), six-axle double-deckers, long after these buses had started to fall out of favour elsewhere on the municipal scene. The six-axle design gave them the look and capacity of trolleybuses but without all the encumbrances such as traction poles and overhead wires. It is believed their appearance on the streets of Leicester was a compromise agreed at a time when there was a lot of pressure on the management to adopt trolleybuses, as had those two other major East Midlands cities, Nottingham and Derby. The last of these vehicles was not taken out of service until June 1958.

Leicester was a pioneer in the move towards reverse livery, from 1962 the traditional colour scheme of deep crimson with cream relief, being changed so that cream became the dominant colour and crimson relegated to relief.

Leicester took delivery of its first rear-engine Leyland Atlanteans in 1963 yet the undertaking remained loyal longer than most other municipal operators to open-platform buses, ordering them as late as 1968. One-man operation of the Atlanteans was introduced in 1971.

In 1972 Leicester joined forces with Midland Red to operate two routes from the borough into the suburbs of South Wigston and Wigston Magna, the first major venture by the corporation outside the boundary. Another cross boundary service was introduced in 1976, extended to Oadby in 1980, along with a jointly operated works service from Braunstone Frith to Oadby. In August 1979 the corporation took over the long-established business of Gibson Brothers of Barlestone, who were trading as 'Comfort Coaches'.

At its peak, in 1953, the fleet had grown to 236 vehicles but this dipped to below 200 when the undertaking reached its nadir in 1968. However, by the 50th anniversary of municipal operation the number of vehicles had gone back up to 216. And in April 1974 Leicester took delivery of the first of 43 Anglo-Swedish Metropolitans – although due to local government reorganisation they would no longer be branded "corporation" buses.

Derby operated its first motorbus in 1924. Other routes followed and when returns proved favourable against those of the trams, it was decided, in 1929, to abandon the latter.

However, trolleybuses were becoming Derby's favoured mode of replacement and the town was granted parliamentary powers to extensively introduce these. Consequently, many tram replacement and new services were trolleybus-operated but motorbuses were used in locations where the electric vehicles were not considered suitable and their usage, as percentage of the total, gradually increased.

Still, for a town (as it was then) of fairly moderate size, Derby was a relatively big trolleybus operator and in 1955 the council drew up plans for extensions along Ashbourne, Uttoxeter and Mansfield Roads, but concerns about wires and traction poles in open countryside brought inevitable objections and led to a public inquiry.

Consequently route extensions were by motorbuses – to Boulton Lane Estate and St. Andrew's View via Perth Street in 1955; to Lyttelton Street and Scarborough Rise in 1958, being examples.

Eight trolleybuses were purchased in 1960 but these proved to be the last as cutbacks in the system commenced two years later, even though official returns showed trolleybus operation to be significantly cheaper than that of motorbuses. Trolleybus services were mainly cross-town although some terminated outside Midland Station, where there was a large turning circle. Any visitor new to Derby, and leaving the station for the first time, would have been in no doubt where he was when confronted by a trolleybus, in dignified olive green and cream, and bearing the legend DERBY CORPORATION in large gold script.

But these days were numbered for by 1964 the Kingscroft and Burton Road trolleybus routes had been abandoned, followed in 1966 by the Sinfin Lane and Wyndham Street services. Scheduled services on the Uttoxeter Road, Victoria Street, Cavendish, and Midland Station sections were withdrawn in November 1966, although, with the wires remaining in place the occasional full service and works services continued to operate infrequently due to staffing difficulties until 9 September 1967.

Prior to the abandonment scheme being put in place, trolleybuses made up close to half of the 165-vehicle fleet.

In May 1969, Derby's traditional dark green livery, which had been used by the corporation since 1904, was replaced by a somewhat nondescript blue and gray, no doubt reflecting the changing times.

Meanwhile, more co-ordinated bus services between the corporation and Trent Motor Traction were once again introduced to supplement three introduced over 20 years earlier; these included long-established Trent routes including the Allestree and Darley Abbey Circulars. Eventually an agreement was reached in 1979 whereby all services were co-ordinated throughout the city, with 83 per cent of them being run by the local authority and 17 per cent by Trent.

In December 1973, Derby Corporation took over the long established business of Blue Bus Services of Willington, four months before the world "Corporation" passed into history and the undertaking was given the new, somewhat emasculated name of Derby Borough Transport in line with local government reorganisation.

THE CORPORATION BUS

For a relatively small municipality, **Chesterfield** provided a lot of bus. Despite having a population of only *circa* 75,000, at the beginning of the 1960's the fleet stood at approximately 130 vehicles, which meant the undertaking was just within the top 40 of the municipal pecking order.

Chesterfield introduced trams in 1901 and these remained dominant until 1925 when the first bus service was inaugurated. Thereafter the pattern was much the same as in most of the smaller undertakings across the country, with buses initially serving new housing areas but eventually taking over completely from the trams, the last of which ran on October 1933.

Trolleybuses had been introduced in 1923 on a cross-town route between Brampton and New Whittington but there was no appetite for expansion and this service closed in March 1938.

Motorbus services operated from the town centre, particularly Vicar Lane Bus Station, which meant that Chesterfield boasted a large number of separate route numbers in addition to its sizeable fleet. Slight variations or deviations of main services were also given separate numbers, which added to the tally.

There was one long distance service (to Sheffield) but other communities some way beyond the borough boundary, such as Bolsover and Clay Cross (infamous for its municipal socialism during the 1970s), also enjoyed regular services.

As with many smaller undertakings, the service number pattern could be confusing. A timetable from 1973, the last full year of Chesterfield Corporation Transport, shows services starting off in chronological order but without a number 1; 11 and 12 were to

Sheffield via different roads but the limited stop service to Sheffield was numbered 512. Services 19 to 25 were essentially the one route but took up six separate numbers. Meanwhile a variation of service 27 was numbered not 27A or 28 but 227 (in fact Chesterfield did not use suffix letters for route identification). 'Normal' numbering ended at 61, followed by two services numbered in the series 71/74 and 81/84. Chesterfield also operated 36 works services (many of them to collieries), numbered in the 100 series.

Throughout the life of the bus undertaking the livery was a mid-green with cream relief, and with lining out long after the practice had been discontinued by most other municipalities for reasons of cost. Chesterfield was also one of the last undertakings to stick with 'old style' municipal branding on the lower side panels of its buses: the words 'Chesterfield Corporation' formed an arc over the coat of arms with 'Transport' set in a horizontal line below the arms – and very impressive it looked too.

At the southern end of the region is **Northampton** – in the heyday of the corporation bus the bootmaker to the nation – where the first municipal bus service began in 1923.

The corporation's traffic peaked in 1950 when more than 48 million passenger journeys were made on this relatively small system. However in 1951, general manager John Cooper left to take up a similar appointment with the larger Leicester undertaking, leaving his successor, J. A. Fielden, hitherto deputy manager, to guide NCT through the rather more difficult times of the fifties.

Between 1950 and 1960 the number of passengers carried fell by 23 per cent, and staff numbers were cut by 11.5 per cent to 450. Nevertheless, in what appears to have been a remarkably successful balancing act by the manager, bus mileage was reduced by just 2 per cent and the fleet was reduced by only two buses.

In the fifties and early sixties, services were numbered 1 to 25. There were 21 normal routes plus a works route (23). Number 6 had a 6A extension and there was a special extension of main service 7 (to Friars Avenue) further along Towcester Road to the cemetery. Missing numbers were 13 14 and 20. Services 6 7 13 18 and 19 were co-ordinated with United Counties, who used Derngate Bus Station. All NCT services left from the town centre at boarding points in the main commercial streets.

As well as the regular service buses, specials were run in the summer months to Silverstone, Billing Aquadrome and Wicksteed Park.

Vehicle numbers at this time was around 90. Livery throughout the life of the undertaking was red with various sizes of cream relief

For several years after deregulation in 1986 Northampton Transport continued as a council-owned company but in 1993 was sold to Grampian Transport Holdings (later to become First Group). The reason for the sale was to fund the Sixfields Stadium and pay for a major refurbishment of the Abington Park Museum – a measure of how some local authorities latterly valued the municipal transport undertakings of which earlier generations felt so proud.

Over in East Anglia, rural Norfolk never looked like fertile corporation bus territory in the last century any more than it does today but **Great Yarmouth**, a popular seaside resort and lying on the edge of the Broads, catered for a great many holidaymakers and day trippers from the Midlands and Yorkshire, in which case an intensive bus service – at least in the late spring, summer and early autumn months – was seen as a civic requirement.

Although Great Yarmouth Corporation was one of the smaller municipal operators (about two-thirds down the pecking order in terms of fleet size) the undertaking actually operated two unconnected tramways, both of which were opened in June 1902. The principal section focused on the main area of population north of the River Yare while a secondary line south of it (initially company owned but bought by the corporation in 1905) linked Southtown and Gorleston.

When motorbuses were introduced in 1920, Great Yarmouth put its faith in double-deckers (which were purchased second hand from the famous London General Omnibus Company) but single-deckers were purchased to cover the first tramway closure in 1924.

Many years later, Great Yarmouth entered bus industry fame when it operated the first one-man operated double-deck bus after the rules relating to two-person crew were altered in July 1966.

For most of the life of the undertaking, livery was blue and white, which had earlier replaced the tramway maroon and cream.

The Suffolk fishing port of **Lowestoft**, Britain's most easterly corporation transport undertaking, introduced trams on a single cross town route from Pakefield to Yarmouth Road in 1903.

Buses were introduced in 1927 as feeders but in 1931, over two stages, they entirely replaced the tram route although an approximation of it remained the backbone of the small bus network for many years.

The operation was uneventful until falling passenger numbers in the late 1950's led to the council entering into negotiations with Eastern Counties to purchase the undertaking.

Although an offer was made, and Lowestoft was one of the smallest operators in the country with no more than 20 vehicles at its peak, the offer was turned down by the council, who decided to wipe the board clean with an intensive rearrangement of existing services and new routes to areas not previously served. Unfortunately, the latter was objected to by Eastern Counties, who were awarded the services instead, an outcome that did not make the corporation's position any better. However, in March 1974 – less than a month before the end of Lowestoft Corporation - a joint services between the two organisations was agreed, which permitted them both to share the various routes within the agreement area.

Despite the decreasing fortunes of the undertaking, Lowestoft took great pride in its fleet. Buses were painted in a very dark chocolate/maroon with cream on the top panels, and with the words LOWESTOFT CORPORATION TRANSPORT in large script placed above the coat of arms.

When Lowestoft became part of the enlarged Waveney District Council in April 1974, the fleetname was changed to that of the new authority and the town's unique identity with its own transport undertaking was gone.

The joint services agreement between the local authority and Eastern Counties lasted only until March 1976, when most of the services were taken over by the latter. In December 1977 Waveney District Council ceased to operate buses altogether and its remaining services were passed on to Eastern Counties – a sad end

EAST MIDLANDS AND EAST ANGLIA

to one of the more interesting of the smaller corporation bus operators.

The flatlands of East Anglia were an unlikely place for a trolleybus stronghold, yet how else could one describe **Ipswich**, where the first corporation motorbus did not enter service until 1950?

Richard Chandler, first holder of the new post of traffic manager, introduced the first diesel buses on new services to Whitehouse and Maidenhall estates, with the intention of valuating the routes for trolleybus operation later. However, as happened in most other cities and towns where trolleybuses operated, the advantages of flexibility and lack of infrastructure costs, which the diesels held over the trolleys, quickly became apparent.

In 1957 consideration was given to the sale of the transport department to Eastern Counties because of mounting losses. An investigative committee was formed but finally decided that the undertaking should remain in corporation hands.

By 1960 the motorbus fleet overtook the trolleybus fleet in size and the writing was on the wall. In 1961 the routes were shared between buses (MB) and trolleybuses (TB) and were: 1, Bourne Bridge-Electric House (MB); 1B Castle Hill Estate-Maidenhall Estate (MB); 2, Electric House-Priory Heath (TB); 2A, Electric House-Airport (MB); 4, Electric House-Felixstowe Road (TB); 5, London Road, Chantry Estate-Foxhall Heath (MB); 6A, Electric House-Gainsboro Estate (via Duke Street) (TB); 6B, Electric House-Gainsboro Estate (via Clapgate Lane)(TB); 7, Foxhall Heath-London Road, Chantry Estate (MB); 8,Ipswich Station-Whitehouse Estate (MB); 9, Whitton-Rushmere Heath (MB/TB); 9A, Maidenhall

Estate-Castle Hill Estate (MB); 11, Electric House-Sidegate Lane (TB); 12, Chantry Estate-Electric House (MB;) X, Whitehouse Estate-Ipswich Station (MB) and Electric House-Colchester Road (TB).

The last trolleybus ran in August 1963.

At the completion of trolleybus abandonment, the fleet consisted of 62 motorbuses, eight of them single-deckers. Limited expansion took place until 1966 with another five buses being delivered. From 1968 to 1980 the majority of new buses purchased were Leyland Atlantean double-deckers but from 1983 single-deckers became favoured.

Livery was green and cream with the coat of arms (but not the town name) on the lower panels.

9

Wales

Small is beautiful

Although representing the smallest of the three nations comprising the island of Great Britain, on a *pro-rata* basis Wales boasted more municipal bus undertakings – although perhaps not bus numbers - per head of population than either England or Scotland.

Not surprisingly, nine of these were located in heavily industrialised South Wales, although significantly, this number did not include Swansea, the country's second largest town (and since elevated to city status).

Therefore, by far the largest operator was **Cardiff**, the capital city of Wales, where, on Christmas Eve 1920 the corporation started running a bus service from St Johns Square to Monthermer Road; by March 1922 the number of services had grown to four.

By 1928 Cardiff owned 75 vehicles making it the ninth largest municipal bus operator in the British Isles at the time (30 years later it had dropped to 19th place, even though by then the fleet had grown to around 260). However for the time being the tram continued to dominate local passenger traffic and bus service numbers,

THE CORPORATION BUS

when introduced, started at 21 to separate them from the trams.

Expansion of the bus system was largely as a result of buying out local private operators, many of whom seemed to be quite entrepreneurial, despite eventually selling out. One former rival, in addition to building bus bodies and running bus services, was in the business of house construction as well.

Improvements to motorbus design and operation led William Forbes, appointed manager in 1928, to recommend complete replacement of the tramway system by motorbuses. This was initially accepted by the transport committee but, aided by an energetic campaign in the local press, a strong body of councillors pushed for the introduction of trolleybuses, on the basis that these vehicles, like the trams, could be indirectly powered by South Wales coal.

This argument won the day and the intention of the full council was for trolleybuses to completely replace trams and become the dominant form of street transport in the city thereafter and Mr Forbes – whatever his personal misgivings may have been – set about planning a system which, if implemented, would have been second only in size to that of London.

Meanwhile, conversion of the tramway system began in 1936, but this was not completed until February 1951 by which the remaining trams were in an extremely worn condition.

The first trolleybus service was launched in 1942, although wartime restrictions initially restricted the grand plan to one route. Extensions began in earnest in 1946 from when, until 1955, the system gradually built up to a peak of 18 route miles – well short of what had been originally planned. Indeed most trolleybus routes extended no further than the trams they replaced. The exception was the extension of the service from the former Victoria Park tram terminus westward to the giant Ely housing estate, which required the installation of four miles of new overhead. Surprisingly for a trolleybus system, this new route provided Cardiff's electric buses with their one appreciable 'climb'.

Apart from the Ely extension, the growing peripheral estates that were constructed during the fifties and sixties were all served by motorbuses. In 1959 there were 34 services, many of them with alphabetical suffixes, numbered between 1 and 47. The services included joint workings with other municipal authorities, namely Newport, Caerphilly and Merthyr Tydfil. Some Cardiff services that went beyond the boundary were distinctly rural in operation, for example penetrating far into the scenic Vale of Glamorgan.

For all the limitations of trolleybus expansion, seven years elapsed between the last extension and the first contraction in 1962 and for that period these vehicles were a dominant factor of city life, especially in the central area, which every service traversed or terminated at. All Cardiff trolleybuses were six-wheel, three-axle leviathans but unusually were equipped with two staircases, which was believed to speed up boarding and alighting.

Even as the system was contracting, Felix Cunuder, the undertaking's inventive chief engineer, made improvements to the 'frogs' (the equivalent of railway points on the overhead wire where two lines separated) that increased speed at junctions; he also designed a lightweight trolley head with reduced dewirements.

Cardiff eventually abandoned trolleybuses in January 1970 (the fourth last British undertaking to do so). Perhaps because it had persisted with trolleybuses for so long, the corporation was relatively late in introducing rear-engine motorbuses. An order for 32 of them was made in 1966 and the first entered service a year later – nine years after the first appearance of a rear-engine bus on normal public service (in Wallasey).

While the all-motorbus system offered greater flexibility, passenger numbers continued to decline and by 1973, a year before Cardiff Corporation Transport came to an end, the total carried was 45 million – less than half the 105 million in the peak year of 1948/49.

Cardiff livery from the start of the tramway undertaking was crimson lake and cream, which continued into the bus era. In 1972 it was decided to change the colour scheme to an all-over orange although since the department has become an arm's length company, Cardiff Bus, this has been further changed to blue and cream.

With Swansea a corporation bus-free zone, this left **Newport** as the second largest municipal operator in the Principality.

The corporation launched the two first motorbus services in April 1924. Five years later it decided to put forward a bill to operate trolleybuses in place of trams on Chepstow Road but this proposal was abandoned a year later in favour of using motorbuses both here and elsewhere in the town.

The last tram ran in 1938 and its demise brought two new bus routes. During the decade Western Welsh came up with a proposal to operate a joint services agreement in the town but this was rejected by the corporation, which was always independent-minded and expansionist in nature. However, in July 1945 Newport did set up a joint interurban service with Cardiff.

Introduction of a one-way traffic scheme in 1949 and the opening of the Dock Street bus station meant a major rerouting of services through the town centre. Meanwhile new services continued to be added up to 1959 to cater for residents in the growing suburbs such as Gaer Estate, St Julian's Estate and Ringland Estate.

An even bigger change took place in 1960 and this provided a revised service system as follows: 1, Town centre to Christchurch; 2, Newport to Caerleon; 3, Maesglas to Malpas; 3A, Town centre to Brynglas Estate; 4, Western Avenue to Gibbs Road; 4a, Bassaleg Road to St Julians; 5, Newport to Goldcliff; 6, Town centre to Alway Estate; 6A, Town centre to Nash Road; 7, Newport to Llanfrechfa; 8, Town centre to Ringland Estate; 9, Pill (Docks) to Corporation Road; 10, Newport to West Nash Camp; 11, Town centre to Masefield Vale; 12, Town centre to RTB Llanwern; 13, Town centre to Ridgeway; 14, Town centre to Barracks; 15, Town centre to Moorland Avenue; 16, Town centre to Ringalnd Estate (Hendre Farm Drive); 17, Town centre to St Julian's; 30, Newport to Cardiff.

The service list was later added to by the 18, to serve housing at Bettws, which was followed by the19 to improve the existing service to the Ringland Estate.

Until 1937 Newport Corporation buses sported a livery of chocolate with cream roof and window frames. Some experimentation with blue and cream then took place before green became the primary colour. Fortunately the amount of green – unlike in some other under-

THE CORPORATION BUS

takings – was measured and with liberal use of cream relief Newport continued to boast one of the more attractive municipal fleet colour schemes, not just in Wales but in Great Britain as a whole.

During the late 1950's Newport suffered more than most undertakings from staff shortages due to competition from construction jobs at the Llanwern steelworks and then from permanent jobs after that. Nevertheless, in the late sixties, with many other municipal operations struggling, it became renowned for balancing relatively low fares with providing profits, a situation that existed until 1979 until the recession set in. But the undertaking is a survivor and today is one of the few bus companies still in municipal ownership.

Merthyr Tydfil Corporation had never operated the town's tramway (it was run by BET) and launched its first bus service, from the town centre to Aberfan and Treharris, in 1924. Growth was rapid and six services were operating 12 months later. These were gradually increased as the council, using its powers as a licensing authority, sapped the resistance of local independent carriers.

The original livery was maroon and cream but in the early 1950's this was changed to dark red with cream relief. For a while the undertaking prospered and by the dawn of the sixties boasted around 80 vehicles.

One-man operation was introduced on 20th March 1966, when the services to Tower Colliery, Swansea Hospitals and to Tair Twynau were converted, as was the Hoelgerrig route in 1966, the year that the last double-deck buses were purchased. In 1967, the livery was again revised to predominantly cream with red relief for most of the single-deckers, although the double-deckers remained in red with cream relief.

Merthyr Corporation acquired the Merthyr to Cefn Coed and the Merthyr to Trefechan services of Davies of Tredegar in March 1976.

A new white and orange livery was introduced from 1975, but was found to be unsuitable and it was replaced in 1983 by a burnt orange, dark brown and cream livery.

There had been a great political impetus to the operation of municipal bus undertakings in the Welsh valleys and Merthyr was no exception. The corporation transport department last produced a surplus in 1958 and by 1982 fares were meeting only 60 per cent of costs. Deregulation in 1986 made the financial situation even more precarious and unsurprisingly the council owned-company eventually went into administration although perhaps more surprisingly managed to survive as a trading organisation until August 1989.

The last of the South Wales local authorities to inaugurate a bus undertaking, **Pontypridd** Urban District Council, launched its first service, to Rhydfelin, in June 1930 and a trolleybus line – between Treforest and Cilfynydd - emerged the following September.

However the trolleybus system was a small one with little room for expansion and after several deferments, the council, in 1955, eventually agreed to its replacement by motorbuses, which took place in January 1957.

The existing Rhydfelin service was linked to the Cilfynydd service, and the Treforest section became a single-deck route.

The inevitable move to one-man operation also led to a linking of several services previously operated independently. In October 1969, rationalisation of the bus network took place, with Pontypridd taking over sole operation of the route to Glyncoch, while the Porth service was handed over to Rhondda Transport and the Ynysybwl service to Red & White. Pontypridd also relinquished its journeys on the former Jones Brothers routes, which were essentially loss making.

Under local government reorganisation in 1974, Pontypridd UDC became Taff-Ely District Council.

Pontypridd was the fourth largest of the Welsh municipal undertakings with around 50 vehicles at the start of the sixties.

Aberdare was some way ahead of Pontypridd in operating the first trolleybus service in Wales, which was launched in 1914. These were used as feeders to tramway services but the technology used by the trolleybuses was very basic and prone to breakdowns.

Eventually, the trolleybuses were replaced by extensions to the tramway – probably the only example in the UK of trolleybus services being converted to tram operation. However, in the interim, a fleet of motorbuses was purchased as substitutes for the trolleys while the tram extensions were being built and when these were completed the motorbuses were used to launch new services in other parts of the district.

For many years Aberdare livery was maroon with cream relief but following trends elsewhere on either side of Offa's Dyke, cream eventually became the dominant colour. Until one-man operation roughly equal numbers of double- and single-deckers were used.

Aberdare became Cynon Valley on local government reorganisation in 1974.

A bus enthusiasts' delight was the **West Monmouthshire** undertaking, which was operated by Bedwelty and Mynddislyn urban district councils

What attracted their attention was the Bargoed Hill route, which involved a climb of 1 in 4.25 and required a succession of specially built buses to operate it over the years, which were always worked by a panel of eight specially trained drivers.

West Monmouthshire began operations in 1925 when the two councils obtained 17 vehicles from local independent operators and used this as the nucleus of a 10-route system.

For many years the livery was red and white but in 1971 this was changed to a very attractive sky blue with light relief.

The undertaking became Islwyn Borough Transport in 1974.

The honour of owning the first municipal motorbus in Wales went to **Caerphilly,** which received powers to operate them in 1917 but did not exact these until 1920 when it began operation of services to Sengheydd and Nelson. In 1922 Caerphilly began a joint route to Trethomas with Bedwas & Machen.

Colours were dark green with cream relief.

Caerphilly, along with Bedwas & Machen and Gelligaer all became part of the new Rhymney Valley undertaking on local government reorganisation in 1974.

Much earlier, **Bedwas & Machen** (which were actually two mining villages) had the dubious distinction of being the only municipal undertaking in Britain to lose its entire fleet in a depot fire, which took place in 1943.

More fortunately, the fleet numbered only three vehicles at the time and after renewal this eventually reached

THE CORPORATION BUS

the giddy heights of five, which took Bedwas & Machen off the bottom of the list of 97 municipal operators in terms of vehicle numbers.

Up until 1947 the fleet had consisted solely of single-deck vehicles, but in November of that year the council purchased two double-deckers from Wigan.

The system was uneventful until 1967 when the Trethomas service was extended to Bargoed, jointly with Western Welsh. Also, the development of the large Graig-y-Rhacca housing estate between Bedwas and Machen, resulted in a second service from Caerphilly to Graig-y-Rhacca via Llanfabon Drive while a third service from Graig-y-Rhacca to the Pantglas Industrial Estate in Bedwas commenced in 1971.

In August 1968, a joint service with Western Welsh, Red & White Motor Services and Gelligaer UDC between Rhymney Bridge and Newport was inaugurated.

Powder blue and white was the main livery sported by this small but highly interesting undertaking.

Gelligaer UDC commenced its first bus service in 1928. Running from Bargoed, which was the centre of operations for Gelligaer UDC, via Gelligaer village, to Ystrad Mynach. The route taken was initially operated by five Leyland vehicles on hire from a local private firm but later that year four new Leylands, this time owned by the council, replaced them.

Livery was red, green and cream, which remained for the lifetime of the undertaking.

In November 1945, the business of Jones Brothers (Treharris) Ltd., was jointly taken over (with Caerphilly UDC, Pontypridd UDC and the West Monmouthshire Omnibus Board), which brought routes from Nelson and Bedlinog, and from Blackwood, to Pontypridd and this largely remained unchanged until August 1968, when a joint service between Newport and Rhymney Bridge, with Red & White Services, Western Welsh Omnibus Company, and Bedwas & Machen UDC commenced.

In 1974 Gelligaer was merged with Caerphilly and Bedwas & Machen to form the transport department of the new Rhymney Valley District Council.

The other two local authority operators in Wales were both on the north coast, many miles away from the municipal heartland in the south. Like several of the South Wales undertakings, however, these were also among the smallest in Britain.

In 1926, on its emergence as an urban district council, **Colwyn Bay** applied for, and received permission, to operate a seasonal summer service in the town. Ten years later, Colwyn Bay became a borough, and the council reacted by stamping the legend 'Colwyn Bay Corporation' on the sides of it coaches, no doubt reflecting local municipal pride in the new status.

This undertaking, which was the smallest in Wales and the second smallest in the United Kingdom, never owned more than half a dozen coaches at any one time. Livery was originally maroon but changed to green and cream, with cream eventually becoming the dominant colour. There was no departmental manager, as such, this role being the responsibility of a traffic manager with the borough entertainments department! (Who says all local authorities are profligate?)

In 1974, along with the Llandudno UDC undertaking, the Colwyn Bay buses passed to the ownership of the new Aberconway District Council.

With sufficient transport operations provided by the Llandudno and Colwyn Bay Electric Railway, and

THE CORPORATION BUS

Crosville Motor Services, **Llandudno** UDC did not apply to operate buses until 1928 and in July of that year the first municipal service, a route along the five-mile Marine Drive, was launched.

The initial fleet consisted of two toast rack vehicles, especially aimed at visitors. A second tourist service was inaugurated in 1950, from Prince Edward Square, travelling via the Little Orme and Gloddaeth Woods to Llanrhos, returning via the West Shore. The following year, a stage carriage service to St. Tudno's Church on the Great Orme commenced. During this decade the fleet size reached its maximum of 17 vehicles. However, although the undertaking was owned and operated by the council, Llandudno never actually boasted "corporation buses" as such - all the vehicles being coaches.

Although modifications were made in 1953 and 1954 the basic route network remained subsequently unchanged.

Livery was maroon and cream until 1968, when this was changed to dark blue and cream.

In April 1974 Llandudno UDC became part of the new Aberconwy District Council, to whom all the bus services and vehicles, including the Great Orme Tramway were transferred.

10

Scotland, N. Ireland, Isle of Man

Over the Border and across the sea

Scotland's attitude to the corporation bus was somewhat enigmatic. Her provincial towns were much less enamoured than their counterparts in England and Wales, and by the start of world war two, all the smaller municipal operators had thrown in the towel, with only the four main cities – Aberdeen, Dundee, Edinburgh and Glasgow – still boasting their own fleets.

On the other hand, the combined population of these cities was in the region of two million, which meant that approximately 40 per cent of the Scottish population either regularly used, or had easy access to, a corporation bus.

What's more, **Glasgow** was the second largest municipal undertaking in the UK and by far the most interesting. By the start of the 1960's the transport department was responsible not just for a large fleet of motorbuses but also the country's third largest municipal trolleybus system, 200 remnants of a 1,100-strong tramcar fleet and a seven-mile underground railway.

Given Glasgow's reputation, in transport circles, as Britain's greatest tram city, it seems hardly surprising

THE CORPORATION BUS

that when the corporation introduced the motorbus (in 1924) it was more than half a century after the first horse trams, 30 years after the start of municipal ownership and 25 years after the start of tramway electrification.

The first motorbus service, worked by single-deckers, was launched in December of that year on a route between Glasgow Green (the city's oldest public park) and Monteith Row. One onlooker, a university student, later penned an essay in which he imagined seeing the landmark vehicle packed with the cheering ghosts of horse bus operators who had been put out of business by the trams half a century earlier. Although fiction, this was to prove remarkably prophetic.

Up to then trams had been so dominant in Glasgow that it seemed nothing could stop their continued expansion and that buses would always be used in a peripheral capacity. In retrospect, however, it is clear that while the Glasgow tramway system had many years of robust life ahead, in mileage terms it had already almost reached its zenith by 1924. There was an extension to Milngavie in the north-west in 1934 and in 1949 a further half-mile of reserved track was laid along Great Western Road, but the main purpose of the latter was as the first stage of a new city-wide light rapid transit system that never came to fruition.

Therefore, from the mid-1920's – with the aforementioned exceptions - all further major expansion of the municipal transport network was carried out by introducing new bus services. Even with literally every major thoroughfare in the city centre served by trams, and tramlines laid on all major arterial roads, buses were still deemed the cheapest and most efficient method of extending public transport links to a growing number of peripheral housing estates, like Knightswood in the west, Sandyhills in the east and Kings Park in the south.

The abandonment of the Uddingston line in 1948, marked the beginning of the end of the Glasgow tram although the closure programme took almost 15 years to complete, the last service running in September 1962.

In 1963, the first full year of bus-only operation, Glasgow Corporation had 64 published motorbus services (with just one gap), although the official figure was deceptively low as it was common practice for several terminal points at either end to share the same number.

From their introduction in 1949, trolleybus services were numbered from 101, on the basis that once tramway closure had been achieved, motorbus service numbers were unlikely to go beyond 100. Eventually eight trolleybus services were operated.

One sense in which Glasgow differed from several other big hitting municipal operators was an almost total absence of city centre termini of any substantial size. A purpose-built stance for south side services 5, 7, 7A, 12 and 31 existed in St Enoch Square. With its main line rail station (up to the Beeching closures of 1966), underground station and airport coach terminal, this was something of a transport hub but, in bus terms, nothing on the scale of the Pier Head in Liverpool or the Piccadilly Gardens area of Manchester. The few other (corporation) bus services that terminated in the city centre were simply turned round at on-street bus stops.

In contrast to the tramway mileage, one third of which was beyond the city limits, corporation buses operated mainly within the boundary, one of the few exceptions being the long, straight cross-city route paralleling the River Clyde which went from Auchenshuggle

THE CORPORATION BUS

in the east, through the city centre and then westward for 10 miles before terminating at Dalmuir, which nudged rural Dunbartonshire. Also, the Glasgow Monopoly area, set up in 1930 to protect the corporation from private (and pirate) bus competition, was not extended later to include Drumchapel and Easterhouse, two huge housing schemes constructed by the corporation during the 1950's following extensions to the boundary. Consequently the nationalised Midland and Eastern SMT buses were able to pick up natural 'corporation' passengers from these boarding points.

The use of numbers to identify bus services was another departure from the heyday of the Glasgow tram. Until the late 1930's, all trams had sported the same lower deck livery, called 'traction orange' with the upper panels painted in one of five colours – red, green, blue, yellow and white, which were used to identify routes. As far as was practicable, no two services sharing a route colour operated on the same street, making it easy for intending passengers (or at least locals familiar with the system) to identify their tram from a distance.

The first double deck buses, purchased in 1930, also sported orange on the lower deck panels but with the upper panels painted in green only. It was decided that colour identification was not practical for bus operation and each bus service was therefore allocated a number, something that was extended to the trams from 1938.

Thus was born Glasgow's almost-unique bus livery of orange, green and cream (with yellow sometimes substituted for orange), which was latterly copied by Halifax, after a demonstrator from Glasgow had trailed in the Yorkshire town. Certainly daring, the new livery nevertheless worried some Glaswegians because they considered the orange and green emphasised the city's religious divide.

Glaswegians genuinely loved their trams, although in referring to them they tended to use the American abbreviation, 'car' (or 'caur' in areas where the parlance was really colloquial), just as their tiny underground was always referred to as 'The Subway'. Therefore, the final procession of Glasgow trams in September 1962 was said to have attracted (in teeming rain) crowds totalling 250,000, a quarter of the city's population at that time.

In contrast, less than five years later barely 200 turned up at Queens Cross terminus, near the Partick Thistle football ground, one Saturday night in May to wave off the last trolleybus – their numbers an eclectic mix of past and present transport professionals; bus enthusiasts armed with cameras and notebooks; and householders from the local tenements who turned the occasion into a wake thanks to their 'carry outs' of whisky and beer chasers (the pubs closed at 10pm in those days).

Alas, the days of the corporation motorbus were also numbered – at least, officially - for in April 1973, Glasgow Corporation Transport (previously Tramways) came to an end after 79 years of service and ownership of the fleet passed to the new Greater Glasgow Passenger Transport Executive. Unlike the situation that applied to the English PTE's, there were no neighbouring municipal fleets with which Glasgow could be enjoined and with the Scottish Bus Group remaining fiercely independent, a system of integrated bus services across the region was never achieved. Therefore, for many years after its closure, Glasgow Corporation Transport effectively stayed as it was, albeit branded as 'Greater Glasgow', followed by 'Trans-Clyde', 'Strathclyde's Buses' and

THE CORPORATION BUS

'Strathclyde Transport' before the 1985 Transport Act finally put an end to any hope of integrated bus services on a region-wide basis.

Many Glaswegians will point a finger to the east and tell you that Edinburghers are 'funny folk' – and they don't mean 'funny, ha-ha' either.

While this author has no wish to enter the age-old rivalry between the two cities, in terms of transport history **Edinburgh** is, to some extent, 'funny, peculiar' in that the corporation actually operated buses before electric trams.

Indeed, for the first two decades of the 20th century, Edinburgh was served by a cable tramway (reputed to be the fourth largest in the world), because of local sensitivity over the appearance of wires and stanchion poles on the streets of the 'Athens of the north'. Environmentally friendly the cable cars may have been but they were slow and subject to frequent breakdowns. Eventually, Edinburgh Corporation decided enough was enough and set about laying an electric system, the first buses being bought in 1919 as a substitute for cable trams, which were not replaced by electric cars until 1922.

In the late 1920's more buses were ordered, this time to act as feeders for the trams or to test potential new tram routes. However, these also coped very admirably on the heavily loaded Easter Road, Holyrood, High Street, Fountainbridge corridor and the advantages of the bus were clearly shown.

During world war two, Edinburgh sustained little physical damage and transport operations soon returned to normal after the end of hostilities.

At first an attempt was made to keep separate, where possible, new bus and existing tram services but as the former grew, duplication became more and more common. Two new bus services started on October 1949, the 24 from St Andrew Sq to Bingham Road and the 25 shuttle from the existing car terminus at Liberton to Burdiehouse but the latter eventually became part of a longer, cross-city bus route.

The first full replacement of trams by buses occurred in June 1952, when the service from South St David St in the city centre to the inner suburb of Comely Bank, was extended (without the cost of track and wires) to the bungalow belt of Craigleith, again showing the cost-effective advantage offered by buses.

Around this time Edinburgh began toying with the idea of operating trolleybuses and in 1953 a Glasgow trolleybus carried out a trial run along Princes Street, one of the booms taking power from the overhead tram wire, with a skate attached to the bus taking return current from the tram rails. However, the corporation did not take the experiment further, despite the fact that several Edinburgh routes involved a number of steep climbs, especially in the southern and south-western areas of the city, where some services terminated almost on the lower slopes of the Pentland Hills.

In 1954, the seven-mile tram service from the GPO to Musselburgh and Levenhall in East Lothian was closed. This was taken over by 'Edinburgh SMT', the regional Scottish Omnibuses company, who agreed not to pick up passengers within the city boundary if the corporation did not operate services outwith it. Thus all mainstream Edinburgh Corporation bus services terminated within the boundary, although an exception was the takeover, in 1956, of a contract service to the airport (which at the time was administratively situated in West Lothian but is now within the boundary of Edinburgh).

By 1957, the first full year of bus-only operation, the system had extended to almost 120 route miles, operating over 46 daytime services numbered from 1 to 49, plus six night services, which became five circulars from October 1960. The first limited stop services were introduced in 1970, the year that also saw the first woman behind the wheel.

Just 120 route miles seems small for an undertaking which, in the early 1960's boasted the sixth largest municipal fleet in the UK, however this probably reflects the situation of Edinburgh Corporation buses being confined by the municipal boundary but operating a dense frequency of services within it.

Vehicle numbers at their peak were just over 700, which included more than 20 coaches, used for city tours and private hire. However, even if one excludes the coaches, Edinburgh could still boast considerably more vehicles than the next-largest municipal operator, Leeds – even though the latter had a larger operating area and a higher population.

Edinburgh City Transport (the terms 'city transport' and 'corporation transport seem to have been frequently interchangeable here) was transferred to Lothian Region, in May 1975. At the time services, with some modification, were still 1 to 49 and there were also several limited stop services numbered 70 to 79.

Dundee had a claim to municipal bus fame in that it was the first local authority in Scotland, and one of the first in Britain, to operate a regular trolleybus service. This was introduced in 1912 and linked Fairmuir Road with the tram terminus at St Mary's. However, because of their ability to throw up dust, the vehicles were not popular with the public (who nicknamed them 'stoories', stoor being the colloquial word for dust) and the service was with drawn in 1914, shortly before the outbreak of World War One. The fact that Dundee councillors and transport officials had gone some years earlier on fact-finding trips to Germany to evaluate trolleybus operation there was purely coincidental.

Meanwhile, the tramway network serving the city of jute, jam and journalism had reached its peak in terms of track length by 1914 so the corporation bus played a prominent part in the lives of local people much earlier here than in the other three main Scottish cities.

The first buses, Thorneycroft single-deckers, arrived in 1921 although ten years elapsed before the first double-deckers entered service.

With the withdrawal of trams in 1956, the corporation purchased 40 retired London buses, a move unpopular with locals who up to then had been used to new-build vehicles. In order to reassure them, the first London Transport RT to be repainted in Dundee livery was displayed in City Square for public inspection. The management were proved to be right and, it would seem, secured a good deal for the ratepayers: only seven years old, these buses gave good service to the city for a further 12 years. These were part of a fleet numbering around 250 vehicles at its peak.

By 1963 Dundee was looking at the new rear-engine buses and a Fleetline from Daimler – the corporation's regular supplier – carried out test runs in May of that year, after which a number of orders followed.

An agreement with the trade unions on OMO operation was secured in 1966 but industrial disputes continued to hamper the undertaking and by 1970, the local Conservative party (much stronger in Dundee than other industrial cities and towns in Scotland) was campaigning for the corporation transport fleet to be taken over by the Scottish Bus Group. However, the idea was eventually dropped.

On the operational front, a comprehensive renumbering of routes took place in 1959, which led to service numbers from 1 to 40, with many starting from and terminating at Shore Terrace and Dock Street in the city centre. These pretty much stayed in place until the undertaking became the property of the new Tayside Regional Council in 1975.

Initially the livery for buses was blue and white (a diversion from trams which were painted in red) but this was changed in green in 1934. During the 'good years' the green was medium in tone, complemented by lining and white relief. Gradually the green darkened and became the all over body colour as well (one assumes to save on painting costs), giving gave the buses a very dull appearance.

However the final delivery of vehicles to the undertaking (obviously for OMO) were painted in a rather attractive two-tone green livery, not unlike that of Leeds, and which were a considerable improvement on the earlier scheme. Thus Dundee Corporation Transport bade farewell with something of a "last hurrah" which reminded the public of their undertaking's earlier, happier days.

Aberdeen, or the granite city, as it is also known, was the most northerly outpost in Britain of the corporation bus.

The first of these ran between Castle Street in the city centre and the fishing village of Footdee on 10 January 1921, later extended to Balnagask Road, Torry. On 30 April 1921, a bus service was started between the Rubislaw tram terminus near Bayview Road and the corporation's newly-acquired Hazlehead Park, to which Aberdonians were starting to flock in droves at weekends.

However, rather than make a bus service permanent, it was decided to double the tram track between Queen's Cross and Rubislaw and extend it from Rubislaw terminus to the interior of the park.

By 1939 there were 111 buses to 102 tramcars, but during world war two, with the number of buses halving through wartime requisition, the trams notably increased their traffic. In 1939, around 41.3 million passengers were carried on the trams, in 1946, 68.7 million. However in the immediate post-war period, the buses quickly regained lost ground, and they provided the services to the later council housing estates of Northfield, Mastrick and Kincorth.

Arriving at the Aberdeen boundary from the south on the A92, and crossing into the city over the Bridge of Dee, a visitor would have immediately come across a joint terminus with corporation tramcar and a corporation bus alongside. The bus served another large housing estate, Garthdee, but was a feeder to the tram service, which took passengers to and from the city centre. However, a special, early morning service carried fish workers direct by bus to Aberdeen Harbour, which was adjacent to the main commercial and shopping area, so the question – why not offer the same service to other passengers at more conventional times of the day? – came to be asked. The operational and financial advantages of moving people from the housing scheme by bus straight into the city centre became apparent and this helped nail the coffin of the tramway system, although critics complained bitterly that with many of the trams new in 1950, their lifetime could have been extended by at least another decade, even if closure was the eventual intention.

In 1958, the year the tram system closed, a further extension was carried out at King Street Garage, which by then hosted the entire 230-strong bus fleet – ironic given that in horse tramway days the corporation at one time had a depot for each route. Aberdeen was later than most municipalities in introducing rear-engine buses, the first of these vehicles not appearing on the grey granite streets until 1967.

By the early 1960's, Aberdeen Corporation was comprehensively serving the city with a simple system of just 18 designated services, numbered 1 to 25 with several gaps, although there were also a number of short workings to Castle Street, just beyond the Town House (the Scottish term for a town hall). As the busy operational 'hub' of the system, this thoroughfare (actually more of a 'square' than a street) had a real buzz about it, especially in the days when it was shared by buses and trams; how sad, quiet and windswept today's Castle Street (inevitably now a pedestrian area) seems in comparison.

In the early 1960's the service pattern was: 1, Balgownie - Garthdee; 2, Auchinyell – Castle Street; 4, Hazlehead – Castle Street or Sea Beach; 8, Summerfield – Cairncry; 9, Springhill or Byron Square – Garden City; 11, Summerhill – Golf Links; 13, Castle Street – Scatterburn; 14, Footdee – Craigshaw; 15/16, Kincorth Circular; 17, Heatheryfold – Torry; 18, Craigiebuckler – Smithfield;

SCOTLAND, N. IRELAND, ISLE OF MAN

20, Marischal College – Tillydrone; 22/23, Northfield – Mastrick; 24; Scatterburn – Airyhall; 25, Hayton – Faulds Gate.

Initially bus livery was a very dark shade of green but a much lighter apple green (with cream relief) was eventually adopted as standard.

In 1975 the undertaking became the responsibility of the new Grampian Regional Council. Aberdeen's coat of arms, with its proud motto, 'Bon Accord', was banished from the vehicles and the fleetname became Grampian, even though this remained essentially a city network and none of the 'regional' buses went within 30 miles of the mountain range from which the new local authority took its name. Weird branding or what?

Belfast, the capital of Ulster was the only place in Ireland where one could find a corporation bus – but the undertaking operated one of the biggest of the UK systems and its bright red colour scheme made sure it boasted some of the best looking vehicles too.

The first buses were painted blue and white (as were the corporation trams) and this prevailed until 1945 when buses were repainted red though the trams retained the original livery, until their total abandonment in 1954.

Belfast took slowly to buses; the first service, from the city centre to Cavehill, was launched in 1920 but a second – this time, cross-city – service did not follow until 1928. The first double-deckers were introduced in 1930, by which time there were still only eight motorbus services compared with 28 tram services. One of the bus services – the number 2, 'Gasworks – Waterworks' - must qualify for the service with the two dullest sounding terminal points in the UK.

As the tramways were run down the bus network expanded by 1973, when the undertaking was taken over by the government-owned CityBus, there were 50 services, numbered between 2 and 93. At its peak the fleet exceeded more than 500 vehicles, around two-fifths of them being trolleybuses.

And it is as a trolleybus, rather than motorbus, operator that Belfast is best known. The first service, to Falls Road, was launched in 1938 and a network of routes developed during and after World War Two.

The high water mark of the network was reached in 1958 when a large one-way traffic system was concentrated on Donegall Square, in the middle of which sits Belfast's impressive City Hall. This effectively turned the square into one huge roundabout and was extremely effective in improving the turnaround in services terminating at the city centre. The result was the densest area of overhead in the UK and to the trolleybus enthusiast, the resultant forest of traction poles and wiring must have been pure sex. However it drew many complaints from less partisan citizens about visual pollution.

The last route extension came a year later when the wires along Falls Road were extended to the Whiterock housing estate. To reach the terminus buses were required to climb a very steep hill and the ability of the trolleys to reach the top without any effort was in marked contrast to the way in which their diesel counterparts struggled up it.

At its height, Belfast, sometimes called 'Titanic Town,' was also a great 'trolleybus town', boasting the largest municipal fleet of trolleys in the United Kingdom, with services radiating north, south, east and west from city centre termini. Among the outer service termini was Stormont, where the wires entered the gates and then proceeded along the approach and right around the graceful parliament building, in effect forming the largest (and most attractive) trolleybus turning circle in the United Kingdom – and perhaps in Europe.

However, just a year after the opening of the city centre one-way system, the corporation decided that the future lay in an all-motorbus system. Stormont and the other routes serving East Belfast were the first trolleybus services to be abandoned in the early sixties and by 1968 only one remained. This closed in May - just four months before the first real stirrings of the civil unrest that was have to such a devastating effect on Northern Ireland for the next 30 years. During that period destruction of vehicles was extensive and, even more tragically, several corporation (and its successor, CityBus) staff lost their lives.

In retrospect the trolleybus era, especially that which stretched from the end of world war two until the closure of operations in 1968, could be seen as a metaphor for the longest period of peace and prosperity since the establishment of the Northern Ireland parliament in 1921. However, no one has gone so far as to suggest that the Troubles could be put down to the demise of the Belfast trolleybus.

The municipal bus network of **Douglas**, capital of the Isle of Man, was extended greatly when in 1949 an Act was passed allowing the corporation to operate buses up to two miles outside the borough boundary, beyond which services had previously not been permitted.

THE CORPORATION BUS

This gave the corporation an administrative problem because at the time, buses operating wholly within the borough boundary did not need a road fund licence, unlike those that operated outside beyond it. As an economy measure only sufficient vehicles required to operate these services were taxed and they carried the letters 'EA' (for Extended Area) next to the fleet number. This practice ceased in 1964 when the need for road fund licences for Douglas Corporation vehicles was removed altogether by the Road Traffic (Public Service Vehicles) Act.

Douglas shared the same problem as seaside resort towns on the mainland - seasonal variability that meant high passenger (and, therefore staff) demand in summer and modest uses during other times for the year. Therefore a relatively large fleet was required to serve a basically small town of around 25,000 and this put a great strain on finances. By the 1950's, when most other undertakings were experiencing an Indian summer, Douglas rarely purchased new vehicles – indeed none at all between 1951 and 1957 and again between 1958 and 1964, when the fleet size stood at 43, 12 of which were single-deckers.

Livery for many years was yellow and red and during the last full year of service – 1975 – there were 17 routes, down from their peak of 21 at the outbreak of war.

On 1 October 1976 the buses of Douglas Corporation were absorbed into the newly formed Isle of Man National Transport Limited, along with those of the Isle of Man Road Services company.

11

Managers and Men

The brains and the brawn

To the contemporary reader the title of this chapter may appear somewhat sexist but it is nevertheless the most appropriate term in the circumstances. The organisations that kept the corporation bus running on our streets were among the most male-dominated sectors of what at the time was a male-dominated society.

At the head of the organisation was the manager, certainly male, and most likely to have been a member of the Institution of Electrical Engineers or, alternatively a Chartered Engineer.

The manager would, possibly, have had a deputy and several senior assistants for each department, although the size of the senior management team would, for obvious reasons, vary depending on the size of the undertaking.

The department would be split into three sections – traffic, engineering and administration. A superintendent would head the traffic section and with him would rest ultimate responsibility for inspectors, drivers and conductors and driver trainers. The upkeep of the vehicles themselves was the responsibility of the chief engineer whose staff included mechanics, fitters, bodybuilders, painters, greasers, cleaners and cleaners. The administrative sector would handle wages and salaries and all personnel issues.

The manager did not enjoy complete autonomy – indeed, far from it. He had to regularly report to the transport committee consisting of elected councillors and aldermen (bailies in Scotland) whose numbers, again, depended on the size of the local authority. The manager had more or less complete freedom with the day to day operation of the buses under his stewardship but major issues – such as buying new vehicles or making major service changes – had to go before the committee for approval. Committee decisions then had to be approved by the full council; mostly they were rubber-stamped but in some cases political infighting took place between the transport committee and the full council, even when members of the same political party made up the majority of both.

A particularly significant example of this occurred in the late 1930's when the transport committee of Manchester Corporation agreed to accept the recommendation of the transport manager, R Stuart Pilcher, that the city should not adopt trolleybuses. However, other councillors thought otherwise, especially when this form of transport seemed to offer much of the benefits of trams with a much lower capital outlay and, anyway, many other cities in England were adopting trolleybuses at that time and they were considered the 'in thing'. Therefore when the full council met to discuss the issue, Manchester voted in defiance of its transport manager and transport committee.

One assumes the manager was not happy with the decision, but did not see the matter as an issue for resignation and set about making the best of what he considered a bad situation. He opened up sufficient trolleybus services to keep the politicians happy but not to the extent that it greatly interfered with his preferred ambition of replacing Manchester's ageing trams with a large fleet of modern motorbuses.

Mr Pilcher seemed to be blessed with that sense of diplomacy that was essential to anyone who aspired to taking charge of a corporation bus undertaking. Managers were in effect forever trying to keep two balls in the air at once – one for running what was essentially a consumer-style business, and one for satisfying the whims and mores of the politicians elected by his customers, the paying passengers. In a not untypical scenario, a manager might be asked to launch a new bus service by a councillor who had been petitioned by his ward residents. If the manager felt that the prospects for such a service looked dodgy in economic terms he had to find a way that would balance commercial reality with social need – and political pressure.

Managers, like every other part of industry, came in all shapes and sizes and with different personalities, which naturally was partially reflected in the operation and branding of the corporation buses under their control.

R Stuart Pilcher seems to have been something an extrovert, as was a later Manchester manager, Ralph Bennett. The latter had an almost meteoric career progression, rising from manager of Great Yarmouth Corporation Transport in 1958 (when it was the tenth smallest municipal undertaking) to chief executive of London Transport within a decade.

Because they played a vital role in keeping the country – and, in particular factory workers - on the move, many of the younger managerial prospects in municipal transport did not serve in the forces during world war two. An exception was Thomas Lord, who during the conflict had served with distinction in North Africa and Italy and was mentioned in despatches. In 1962 he was plucked from the managerial obscurity of Barrow to head the operation at Leeds, and later was elevated to the first director general of the West Yorkshire PTE. In 1966 Albert Burrows was manager at Chesterfield, another smaller undertaking, and three years later found himself director general of Merseyside PTE, via a short spell as manager at Liverpool.

Other managers preferred just to keep their heads down and get on with the job without any attendant publicity. Ironically, even the 'shy' ones had the most recognised of names in the city or town that they worked for because every corporation bus was required to carry legal lettering giving the title and address of the undertaking and the name of its manager. In a period somewhat more formal than today, most managers seemed to prefer using their Christian initials to a full out Christian name.

One interesting feature of the managerial scene was the relatively large numbers of fathers and sons who rose to the top of their trade, on occasions even occupying the same role, albeit at different times of course.

In 1928, as the Birmingham undertaking was beginning its growth to become the biggest 'municipal' in the country, the manager, Albert Baker, retired and was replaced by his son, Arthur, who had joined the transport department in 1906 and eventually rose to be chief engineer. Prior to his retirement, Baker Snr had built up one of the largest tramway networks in the country. Soon, the tramcar began to fall from grace – even in some big cities – and Baker Jnr then went on to dig up the tracks laid down by his father. Sadly, Baker Jnr died in service, three years before the last Birmingham tramcar closure.

Just below Birmingham in the fleet size stakes was Glasgow where the penultimate manager, Eric Fitzpayne (or E.R.L. Fitzpayne, as he was referred to in the legal lettering on Glasgow buses) was the son of Frederick Fitzpayne, a former manager at Edinburgh Corporation Transport, who tragically died at a relatively early age. Fitzpayne Jnr did not enter municipal transport until the age of 26 but by 30 he was manager at South Shields, where he introduced trolleybuses, and in 1937 moved to Glasgow as number two, in anticipation of the retirement of the then transport chief.

South of the Border, another example of the municipal family connection was Ben England, who, after five years in the manager's seat at St Helens from 1928, went on to further his career in the Midlands, being in charge of first Leicester and then Nottingham until his retirement in 1962; his father, Harry, had been manager at Sunderland Corporation during tramway days. Ronald Fearnley, manager at Southend and, later, Coventry, where he spent almost 30 years, started his career in the transport department at Sheffield, where his father, Arthur, was manager up to 1945. Fearnley Jnr is said to have performed miracles in getting Coventry's buses and trams back to near normal within days of the blitz on the city on 14 November 1940.

Some managers were happy to live out most of their professional lives with one undertaking and were none the worse for that. One of these was Frank Lythgoe, who, after moving from Rawtenstall, spent 30 years at

Middlesbrough where under his management the vehicles under his control gained an enviable reputation for appearance and maintenance.

Other aspirants for high office took the view that one had to 'move on to get on' and there was many a managerial wife who no sooner had settled in and made friends in a new environment than her husband came home one evening and announced that they'd soon be on the move again.

R Edgely Cox, whom we have already met, had spells with London Transport, and then Bradford and Bolton corporations before attaining a manager's seat, first at St Helens and then Walsall, where his activities with the town's trolleybus network became legendary. Moris Little began his career as a graduate apprentice in his home city of Edinburgh, and eventually became boss of that city's undertaking – via the managerial chairs at St Helens and then Reading. Ronald Cox (like Mr Lord a war veteran), who set out on his career in his native St Helens, was another frequent flitter before eventually taking charge at Bournemouth (shortly after narrowly failing to land the top job at Leeds). Not long after settling in at Bournemouth, Mr Cox was off again, this time to Edinburgh, which he managed for ten years until, in 1973, he was appointed director-general of the new Greater Glasgow PTE – arguably the top urban public transport position in the country outside London.

With so much coming and going, it was inevitable that some coincidences would crop up. For example, filling the post vacated by Mr Cox at Bournemouth was a young engineer called Ian Cunningham, who only a year before had moved south from Edinburgh – the undertaking that Mr Cox had left Bournemouth to manage.

Much earlier, in 1946, when the (even by then) legendary Stuart Pilcher left the manager's post at Manchester Corporation to take up a regional position in the Midlands, he was replaced by Albert Neal, who had worked under Pilcher until 1938, when he left to take up a senior position with Edinburgh - the undertaking managed by his old boss before moving to Manchester in 1929.

Another coincidence cropped up in 1967 when Ralph Bennett, while manager at Manchester, was formally handed the first of the stylish 'Mancunian' buses ordered from British Leyland. Presenting the vehicle to Mr Bennett was the Leyland chairman, Sir Donald Stokes – whose father, Harry Stokes, had introduced corporation buses to Plymouth as transport manager there more than 40 years before. To further the coincidence, Mr Bennett had himself worked for Plymouth Corporation Transport earlier in his career.

As a result of the frequent movement referred to some undertakings seemed to become 'staging posts' on the road to higher things. One example was Rochdale, from where Chaceley Humpidge moved to manage Bradford, Joseph Franklin to manage Blackpool and the aforementioned Ronald Cox to manage Bournemouth. Mr Humpidge furthered his career by being appointed manager of the Sheffield undertaking in 1961; after retirement he took holy orders but, sadly, died soon after.

In the case of Mr Franklin, the Blackpool transport committee were no doubt impressed by several major achievements he made at Rochdale. By altering fuel pump settings and improving engine conditions he substantially reduced fuel consumption - in 1952/53 £3,000 was cut from the fuel bill despite an extra 10,000 miles being travelled. He also developed an automatic machine capable of washing the top and sides of vehicles at the same time, which meant a bus could be cleaned in five minutes instead of the hour it took under previous methods.

For a few managers, career advancement did not necessarily equate with a bigger position, added security and a fatter pay cheque. Rather than become part of the West Midlands PTE empire, the last manager at Coventry Corporation, Derek Hyde, chose instead to apply for – and secure - the job of manager at Blackpool Transport, even though it involved a drop in salary. The challenge – and with its 1930's built fleet of trams Blackpool would certainly be that – was too great to turn down.

Another municipal manager for whom a senior PTE post was not 'the end' was Geoff Hilditch. After progressively climbing the career ladder in engineering posts with Manchester, Leeds and Halifax corporations and then, as deputy manager at Plymouth, he eventually attained a manager's post, at Great Yarmouth, in 1960 and returned to Halifax in the same capacity three years later. When Halifax became part of the new Calderdale District and the former corporation's bus activities were absorbed by West Yorkshire PTE in 1974, Mr Hilditch became director of engineering and many men close to 50 (as he was then) might have been quite happy to settle for that. But not in this case for Hilditch later chose to become manager of Leicester City Transport (one of the largest municipal survivors not covered by PTE legislation) and even had a short spell as manager of Cynon Valley Transport (the former Aberdare undertaking) in South Wales before taking retirement.

Mr Bennett, as we have already learned, was one of those managers who took a hands-on approach to vehicle design, as did Edgeley Cox and Chaceley Humpidge. In one case this extended far beyond buses: G G Harding, manager at Wallasey in the early 1960's, was a keen exponent of the AVC or hover vehicle – a land-based equivalent of the hovercraft – and built nearly 30 experimental rigs. In one paper written in 1964 he speculated about a future in which high speed hover vehicles, propelled by linear induction motors, with road wheels for use when off track, could obtain speeds approaching those of aircraft while retaining the normal function and mobility of wheeled vehicles at terminal points

Unless an elected councillor and member of the transport committee, the only role for women in the corporation bus era was in a relatively down table position within the transport offices (secretary to the manager was considered a prime post) or, of course, on the buses themselves as conductresses. Even here it wasn't always easy. Women conductors were common during world war two with so many men serving in the forces but as soon as peace came, the females were expected to leave their jobs to make way for the returning menfolk. However the mass unemployment which occurred shortly after the end of world war one did not repeat itself in the mid- to late-forties and corporations began, somewhat reluctantly, to hire women again, although some would not employ those who were married. Although females were permitted to drive trams (and in some cases trolleybuses also), the cab of the motorbus remained a no-go area for a long time and only in the last years of the corporation bus era did women start to be seen behind the wheel.

In many undertakings the crews, whether all male or male-female, worked as a team, sometimes over many years; instinct helped them develop as an efficient combination and the service that they provided – in terms of timing, fare collection and passenger satisfaction – was enhanced as a result. On occasions, male-female partnerships would blossom into romance and, eventually, marriage although romance could also have its downside if it occurred – as it sometimes did - when the bus driver or his conductress (or both) were each married to someone else!

Many who joined as conductors eventually qualified as drivers and went on to give long years of service. Others, however, simply took on the role because they were 'between jobs, and hiring and maintaining suitable staff numbers was a constant headache for managers from the mid-1950's onward.

The manager of one of one large undertaking, in a report to his transport committee in 1951, said that of a traffic staff complement of more than 1,000, over half had been in the service of the department for less than a year, while less than 10 per cent had had 20 years service – a perfect example of how drivers (and, in particular conductors), 'came and went' with depressing regularity.

There was, however, one compensation for management: although transport departments were 'unionised' the transient nature of the job for many drivers and conductors meant that strikes were relatively rare even though a few undertakings – Liverpool and Dundee, in particular – had a bad reputation for staff militancy.

Many conductors – especially female ones – were well known for their repartee or their ability to put down drunk, aggressive or impertinent passengers; but they also had to balance this with a certain amount of diplomacy because most of their passengers were ratepayers and, at the end of the day, the 'shareholders'.

One male conductor with the 'gift of the gab' was Irishman Michael Naughton who one day while working his shift on a Swindon Corporation bus took the fare from a pretty young passenger, Sheila McLeod, and plucked up the courage to ask her for a date. They married two years later and in 2003 celebrated their 50th wedding anniversary by which time they had children, grandchildren and great grandchildren. Mr Naughton later became a driver and ended his 40-year career with Swindon Corporation Transport as chief inspector.

Another long server was Ernest Smith, a driver with Rochdale, who in 1960 briefly achieved national fame as the first person to win the National Road Safety trophy. To do so, he had to beat off a formidable challenge from 15 other finalists from an original list of more than 100 nominees, all of whom, in their own way, had saved children's lives.

Although child road casualties are still a serious problem it was much worse in those days - in 1959 630 children had been killed, and 5,200 injured, on Britain's roads.

A three-foot high silver crystal trophy, donated by Shell-Mex and BP Ltd, was presented to Mr Smith by the transport minister, Ernest Marples. The day after receiving the award, Mr Smith returned to Manchester Victoria station to be greeted by the chief constable and his own boss, the corporation's publicity-minded transport manager, Ronald Cox and members of the town council and the road safety committee.

THE CORPORATION BUS

Always known as 'Safety Smith', he retired in 1977 after 33 years as a driver with Rochdale Corporation.

Collecting fares was considered the lesser of the two jobs and conductors were paid less than drivers. However in one respect conducting had a distinct advantage, at least on double-deckers: one study in the early 1970's – compiled before the perfection of power steering - found that the average heart attack rate among conductors (who ran up and down stairs countless times during a shift) was about one-fifth that of their sedentary colleagues behind the wheel.

In the days of the half-cab bus, drivers were isolated and therefore immune to all the human activity that was going on behind them but their job wasn't particularly easy. Crews were given summer and winter uniforms, the latter usually including a heavy woollen overcoat. However, unheated cabins still made the driver's job uncomfortable on cold days and nights, especially in the hilly routes of Yorkshire and Lancashire. Bus drivers of that era have written of wearing bicycle clips on their trousers, to try and help keep out the cold. No doubt mass-produced, inexpensive women's tights – had they been widely available at the time – would have benefited them even more in combating such conditions. But it is hard to imagine your typically traditional (small 'c') conservative municipal transport manager authorising these as part of the official uniform!

12

Oozing Civic Pride

Branding and identity

Just what was it that made the corporation bus not just different but that bit superior as well?

It wasn't design or performance because most corporation buses were basically no different from those vehicles owned by nationalised and private rivals operating in urban environments.

The answer, rather, could be found in local community ownership, identity and branding, which above anything else made the corporation bus stand out from those of other operators. Company buses in some towns (Aldershot, Barnsley and Mansfield spring to mind) also used local branding but nothing could beat the city or town fleet name, municipal title and – most important of all – the coat of arms, which was the trademark of every corporation fleet.

Corporation buses usually had a superior livery scheme too, especially after nationalisation of the many company fleets in 1948, after which these buses began sporting a bland, national overall green, later replaced by red. The exception was north of the Border where the Scottish Bus Group, equivalent to the National Bus

THE CORPORATION BUS

Group in England, allowed its various operational subgroups much more individuality in livery and branding, much of which retained a traditional element.

Red and green were also the dominant municipal colours but, unlike the nationals, these came with a wide variety of shades, relieved by varying levels of white or cream. Towards the end of the 1960's, cream became the more dominant colour in several undertakings.

Because individual tastes differ, colour is a subjective issue but Accrington was at or near the top of many an enthusiast's list of favourite colour schemes. Red and dark blue do not go naturally together but in this small Lancashire mill town it seemed to work. The colours were those of the 1st Lancashire Fusiliers, for whom many local men volunteered on the outbreak of world war one and who suffered terribly in the first day of the Battle of the Somme in July 1916. The addition of black on the bus window frames is said to commemorate that sad day.

As Accrington showed, some of the best liveries were to be found among the smaller undertakings, such as Lowestoft, which sported a dignified combination of chocolate/dark brown (lower) and cream (upper). How similar sized towns without their own municipal buses must have envied Lowestoft having its identity stamped in this manner – at least until the undertaking became somewhat of a drain on the rates.

The buses of Maidstone, another small undertaking, were equally impressive with their ochre (light brown) livery although this was latterly replaced by a somewhat insipid blue and white.

Bournemouth's buses were admired by people from many parts of the country, because it boasted a large and

OOZING CIVIC PRIDE

impressive trolleybus network and the 'garden city' image of this pleasant but bustling seaside resort seemed to be reflected in the yellow (primrose) livery, which was relieved in a dignified manner by maroon.

Blue was popular in the West Midlands, being used by Birmingham (with cream), West Bromwich (dark and light blue) and Walsall (all over blue). Neighbouring Wolverhampton (apple green and canary yellow) was the exception here.

In Scotland the liveries of the nationalised buses (Alexanders, Northern Bluebird, etc) were often thought to be superior to the municipal ones. The Scottish exception was Edinburgh, where the madder (a mixture of maroon and red) and white colour scheme seemed to be exactly the right choice for this grey but dignified capital city. By contrast, Dundee's medium-dark green was depressingly sombre; Aberdeen boasted a more pleasant apple green, spoiled by grim grey roofs; overall the livery was much less impressive than its predecessor, a very sombre but impressive dark green, which from a distance could almost be mistaken for black.

Following the appointment of a new manager, several undertakings had a change of livery half way through their existence, with Liverpool, Salford, Blackpool and Sunderland among those dropping red in favour of green and Newport changing from chocolate to green. Chester went the other way and changed from green to red. Sometimes this was done because the manager had a preference for a particular colour or to avoid a colour clash with a rival company operator. Latterly colour changes were driven by the need to cut down on the costs of repainting.

While livery was important, it was the coat of arms that was the *piece de resistance* of the corporation bus, even invoking a sense of local pride among people not normally disposed towards municipal government and its various departments. The arms were almost always placed in the middle of both lower side panels, and also on the upper panels on buses belonging to those undertakings that shunned external advertising almost up to the end – or right up to the end in the case of Middlesbrough, Stockton and Wigan.

The branding of the town or city name differed from location to location. Before world war two, some undertakings (Hull and Dundee for example) had the name painted in giant script across the upper panels but this gradually fell out of use. By 1960 a growing number of municipalities – among them the four Scottish ones – were content to use the coat of arms without script. This was also true of Birmingham although one of its neighbours continued to the end with WEST BROMWICH CORPORATION in relatively large script just below the lower window panels. The most common usage of script was to have the town or city name followed by 'Corporation Transport' or simply 'Corporation' placed above or below the coat of arms (e.g. Derby and Colchester). Newcastle upon Tyne, by contrast, preferred to copy the capital city by condensing the title to 'Newcastle Transport' – which was also designed in script in the style of London Transport too. This was somewhat ironic given that the full title of the undertaking was the rather long-winded 'Newcastle upon Tyne Corporation Transport and Electricity Department'.

After being branded with 'Manchester Corporation' for many years, the title on that city's buses was changed to 'City of Manchester' (placed below the coat of arms), finally becoming 'Manchester City Transport'. For most of its last two decades, Liverpool seemed content with the coat of arms on the lower side panels – in contrast to the tramway heyday when the famous 'green goddesses' were branded 'Liverpool Corporation Passenger Transport' in large script, with the words enveloping the coat of arms within an oval. Near the end, the buses started sporting 'City of Liverpool' in addition to the city crest – a last act of defiance perhaps?

In Bradford and Salford a new manager changed the name of the undertaking from 'Corporation Transport' to 'City Transport'. This led to very impressive branding in the case of the former with 'Bradford City Transport' placed above the coat of arms, but with 'Bradford' in much bigger script than the rest of the title, so that from a distance what stood out was the arms and city name. South Shields went a step further and used only the town name with the coat of arms – which again looked very impressive. Huddersfield was a rare exception in not always placing the coat of arms on the side panels of its red buses – preferring the front panel instead.

Most corporation bus services were identified by numbers although several (Exeter, Oldham and Preston among them) at one time used only letters then a combination of numbers and letters, while Middlesbrough stuck with letters exclusively throughout the life of the undertaking, with the exception of a joint service with neighbouring Stockton. Some smaller systems (e.g. Maidstone and Widnes and several in South Wales) managed to get by without numbers or letters and confined themselves to destination screens.

Service numbering could at times seem complicated. Some undertakings grouped numbers in blocks of ten, which meant that the highest number was far in excess of the number of services worked – e.g. services 20, 21, 22 and 23 might be followed by 30 to 35 after which the next service number would jump to 40. Although Derby operated a service 61 this did not mean that the network actually boasted 61 services – 61 was simply a deviation of main line route 6. Most operators would identify a route deviation or variation with a suffix letter ('A' if there was one route deviation, 'B', 'C', etc if there were more) next to the number.

One transport historian once suggested that some of the small-to-medium undertakings liberally used high numbers simply to give the impression of being much bigger operations than they really were. In some smaller undertakings, however, the use of a high route number was necessary to prevent clashing with lower numbers already in use with other operators working locally or sharing another operator's number on joint workings.

In contrast to the situation in England, the Scottish municipalities used a simple – and perhaps more honest -chronological system: if gaps existed in the list of services, a new service would be allocated one of the 'unused' numbers – if not it would be given the number immediately above highest that already existed. That said, numbering was much simpler for municipal operators north of the Border because joint workings with other operators did not exist in Scotland.

On local government reorganisation in 1974, several more county boroughs in England became metropolitan districts while the others were classed as non-metropolitan districts. In the former, transport operation became the responsibility of the relevant passenger transport executive, where it had not already done so. By contrast, non-metropolitan districts in many instances had their boundaries greatly expanded although their functions were reduced. One of these functions was public transport, with the districts given responsibility for operating buses, if already owned, but the county council becoming the transport authority. From then on 'Corporation' dropped from usage on the exterior of buses, to be replaced mostly by the boring and bland 'borough' or, worse still, 'district' council, even though these authorities were no longer boroughs in the accepted sense. Fortunately there were a few welcome exceptions, among them Nottingham City Transport and Plymouth City Transport.

After deregulation in 1986 it should have been perfectly possible for the remaining municipal undertakings to revive 'Corporation' in branding terms because these new arms-length council companies were free to call themselves what they liked, so long as this did not interfere with anyone else's copyright. That none of them did so was no doubt caused by a feeling that the word 'corporation' by that time appeared out to date – strange given that the 1980's have since gone down in history as the great retro decade of the 20th century.

13

All Wired Up

The trolleybus towns

With the notable exception of Liverpool, Sheffield and Edinburgh, the big corporation transport undertakings – and more than a few of the smaller ones too – operated trolleybuses at one time or another.

With some undertakings, the trolleybus played a big and, at times, dominant, role. At the start of the 1960's, Belfast boasted the country's largest municipal trolleybus fleet, while Bradford operated the highest level of route mileage beneath two wires. In relation to the size of the communities they served, Ipswich, Darlington, South Shields, Huddersfield and Wolverhampton were even bigger trolleybus operators, on a *pro rata* basis at their respective peaks.

On the other hand, in the case of Manchester and Glasgow, two of the biggest overall operators, the trolleybus remained peripheral to the motorbus service core. Glasgow trolleybuses did penetrate George Square – the civic heart of the city – but their journey through the central area was usually by way of secondary streets, devoid of big stores or major office buildings. In

Manchester, trolleybuses terminated in the central area but there were no services through the main shopping thoroughfare of Market Street. Indeed, given that Lancashire boasted by far the most corporation bus undertakings of any county in the country, its local authorities were strangely lukewarm towards the trolleybus, the only other municipal operator of this vehicle by 1960 being Ashton-under-Lyne.

Initially, the trolleybus had promised so much, technical advancements in the early 1930's making it an attractive and cost effective alternative to the trams, especially as most corporations were facing the prospect of expensive track renewal and repair. Another factor in their favour was that trolleybuses would continue to provide 'load' for the local power station, which invariably was also owned by the local authority.

At the end of world war two it was presumed that trolleybus expansion would continue where it had left off at the start of the conflict; indeed, Cardiff had launched its first route in 1942 and in 1949 Glasgow opened what grew to be Britain's third largest system; but it also proved to be the last.

A major catalyst for a change in attitudes was the nationalisation of the electricity supply industry in 1948, which led to councils losing control of power generation and much of the local political impetus for trolleybuses was also lost as a result. On the other hand, there was still the beguiling prospect of cheap nuclear power and most cities and towns who were operating trolleybuses at the end of the war continued to make extensions, albeit more reservedly than had earlier been anticipated.

The big body blow came in 1954, with the decision by London Transport to abandon its trolleybus system – at the time the largest in the world – in favour of motorbuses, in a programme to be completed over an eight-year period to 1962. This badly affected the morale of Britain's remaining trolleybus supporters among transport professionals; more practically, the London decision saw British manufacturers withdraw from building trolleybuses, leaving the surviving municipal trolleybus systems increasingly reliant on spares and rebuilds.

Still, even as the 1960's dawned there were plenty of trolleybus strongholds, only Brighton and Portsmouth having announced total closure at this stage. Indeed, the Bournemouth, South Shields and Huddersfield fleets all consisted of more trolleybuses than motorbuses while in Bradford and Wolverhampton the situation was roughly 50-50.

If the above factors in themselves were insufficient to kill off the British trolleybus, what finally did for it was the planned rebuilding of town and city centres. With their fixed routes, trolleybus services became increasingly difficult to operate around and through massive construction sites, with the result that trolleybuses came to be seen as an encumbrance, even among lukewarm supporters and neutrals.

Another negative factor was the way in which trolleybuses were prone to de-wirement, especially at busy junctions, to avoid which some drivers had to negotiate at speeds of no more than 5 mph.

Consequently, of the 23 trolleybus systems operating at the start of the 1960's, all were gone just over a dozen years later.

An early 1960's casualty was Ipswich, abandoned in 1963, even though this undertaking had been 'all trolleybus' as late as 1951, has had Darlington but whose trolleybus system closed even earlier, in 1957. Neither could the connection with power generated by Durham coal save the South Shields system, which closed in 1964; across the Tyne, the large Newcastle network was completely run down from its peak in 1963 in just three short years, ending in 1966 – the same year as Nottingham, which had been so enthusiastic about trolleybuses back in the 1930's that for a short period it boasted the largest network in the country. One year later, Nottingham was followed in completing its abandonment plans by another Midland big hitter, Wolverhampton, and the smaller Derby

Even Reading, whose citizens in 1964 were told that trolleybuses "were here to stay", said goodbye to its trolleys just four years later. The following year trolleybus operation in Southern England came to an end with the closure of the Bournemouth system, much loved by locals and the town's many visitors alike. This left trolleybus operation confined to Walsall, Cardiff, Teesside and Bradford.

Some of the abandonment programmes were so severe and carried out with such questionable speed that vehicles with years of life left in them were sent for scrap. Bradford, Britain's pioneer trolleybus operator, announced its intention to abandon in 1961 but in a more measured way that was the case elsewhere. Consequently, the life of the system was extended by more than a decade so that the last trolleybus run in Bradford – and in public service anywhere in Britain – did not occur until March 1972. Unlike most other trolleybus closure ceremonies, the one at Bradford was attended by large crowds of well-wishers and as the last vehicle passed City Hall, the bells played *Auld Lang Syne*.

Managers were generally split into 'pro' and 'anti' trolleybus camps. Those against felt that nothing could beat the 'independent unit' (i.e. the motorbus), a claim made by the transport manager at Newcastle Corporation as far back as 1906 when trams ruled the urban road. The opposite view was that the more mileage in a system was given over to trolleybuses, the cheaper they became through economies of scale. The performance of trolleybuses was particularly effective on hills and another asset was regenerative breaking which meant that when the driver put his foot on the brake pedal, 'lost' power was returned to the overhead wires via the booms (trolley poles). The ability of the trolleybus not to belch out fumes was not such a big issue in the 1950's and 60's but would certainly be welcomed by large sections of the population nowadays (particularly mothers with babies and young children seated at 'car exhaust level' in buggies).

Some managers, as seems natural, simply changed their minds. When appointed as manager at Newcastle in 1949, Frank Taylor inherited a large trolleybus system and spoke out against those who called for their replacement by motorbuses. By 1962, however, he was proposing the abandonment of trolleybuses in Newcastle and once approved by the corporation, he carried out the task with remarkable efficiency!

Warnings from trolleybus supporters were also given about over-reliance on the supply of oil – which turned out to be prescient given that just over a year after the final closure, at Bradford, the Yom Kippur War in the

Middle East had major repercussions for the supply and price of oil and whose effects are still with us.

Attitudes among the travelling public also differed from location to location. Huddersfield citizens were very proud of their trolleybuses, as were those in Bournemouth, where trolleybuses were described as the "silent service" but Glaswegians (who much preferred their trams) nicknamed them the "silent death".

In reality, trolleybuses had an excellent safety record – as much so in Glasgow as elsewhere, although a somewhat bizarre accident did take place within the Scottish system and because it involved an international diva the incident received banner headlines.

In the winter of 1966 the American singer, Dionne Warwick, was on a tour of Britain, which included a gig at the Odeon cinema in Glasgow city centre. While she was performing a thick fog had descended over the Clyde Valley and when the singer emerged from the stage door in West Nile Street – a secondary thoroughfare gloomy at the best of times – a real 'pea souper' had settled. Crossing the road a few moments later Ms Warwick sustained a leg injury from a trolleybus making its way north on route 106. The singer sued Glasgow Corporation Transport and its manager, Eric Fitzpayne, but when the matter was eventually settled out of court, the usual confidentiality clauses applied.

The incident obviously did not do any long term damage to Ms Warwick's career, which went from strength to strength, proving that she was much more robust than any Glasgow trolleybus. In the year following this incident, the city bade farewell to the last of these high-acceleration, silent and fume-free vehicles. *Anyone Who Had A Heart* would surely weep.

Municipal trolleybus operators in the United Kingdom as at 1 January 1960: Ashton-under-Lyne, Belfast, Bournemouth, Bradford, Brighton, Cardiff, Derby, Doncaster, Glasgow, Huddersfield, Hull, Ipswich, Maidstone, Manchester, Newcastle upon Tyne, Nottingham, Portsmouth, Reading, Rotherham, South Shields, Teesside, Walsall, Wolverhampton. At that time only Brighton and Portsmouth had made a decision to completely dispense with trolleybuses.

14

Missing Municipals

Buses were not their thing

Although most cities and large towns in the United Kingdom boasted their own corporation bus fleets, there were, nevertheless, also a few major exceptions to the rule.

The biggest of these was Bristol, in 1960 the eighth largest city in the country and unofficial capital of the West Country.

The reason for Bristol's absence from the corporation bus story goes back to the start of the tramway era, indeed to 1871 when a clause in the Tramways Act gave local authorities the option of taking over the emerging company-owned systems every seven years. In similar sized cities the local authority eventually exercised that right but for some reason Bristol continued to dither every time the opportunity came up.

Understandably, with the sword of Damocles hanging over its head every seven years, the privately-owned Bristol Tramways and Carriage Company was reluctant to invest in new stock with the result that by the late 1930's - while places like Liverpool, Sheffield and Glasgow were launching Art Deco-influenced designs of

THE CORPORATION BUS

tramcar, Bristol's trams were still open toppers of the type which had been around at the turn of the century.

A third party – in this case Nazi Germany – brought the city's tramcar dilemma to an end when a massive bomb hit the powerhouse and closed the system for good in April1941. However, by that time, the company had built up a fleet of modern buses and although the corporation did not have any ownership rights, councillors served with company representatives on a joint board whose operating responsibilities covered the city and immediate surroundings.

Still autonomous and in local hands, the company buses carried a very individualistic branding, which included a very attractive livery comprising dark blue and cream, not unlike that of Birmingham. They also carried the coat of arms and city title on the lower panels, therefore any stranger arriving at Temple Meads station must have readily inferred that Bristol was a fully fledged operator of corporation buses.

However nationalisation of the company in 1948 brought big changes. It still retained operating autonomy but the local blue livery was changed to nationalised overall green; then the coat of arms went, and the very name, Bristol.

During the 1930's some of the smaller tram-operating municipalities used the closure of their systems to hand responsibility of local transport over to private bus companies, while others continued as bus operators but then sold out after a few years. One of these was Gloucester where, for many years under company ownership, the former municipal the fleet retained local livery and carried the coat of arms, so to the uninitiated they still had that 'corporation look' about them. Among

MISSING MUNICIPALS

other municipal bus operators who sold out before world war two were Kilmarnock, Perth, Keighley and York, although the latter operated jointly with West Yorkshire for several years.

Like Bristol, another large city that eluded the corporation bus was Stoke on Trent, although this may be due in part to the fact that the latter did not become a combined city until 1910 and local loyalties were still concentrated very much on the six independent-minded towns that made up the new authority – Hanley, Stoke, Burslem, Tunstall, Fenton and Longton. Still, after an uneasy start, Stoke on Trent Corporation gradually built up a good relationship with the Potteries Motor Traction Company, which became the mainstay of local transport and whose distinctive overall red livery provided local branding for more than 60 years after the last trams ran in 1928.

Another sizeable exception was Norwich, where, as in Bristol, trams had remained in company ownership, a situation that continued with the changeover to buses in 1935.

Even in the municipal stronghold of Yorkshire, Barnsley, Scarborough and Wakefield councils did not operate corporation buses. In the case of the latter this probably led to Wakefield being chosen (over Leeds, Bradford, Huddersfield or Halifax) as the location for the headquarters of the West Yorkshire Passenger Transport Executive in 1974, because of its 'neutrality'. By contrast, on the other side of the Pennines there was no Lancashire municipality of any appreciable size that did not run its own buses.

In the Midlands, non-municipal operators included relatively large towns like Rugby, Stafford and

Worcester, no doubt due in part to the extensive network of local and inter-town services provided by Midland Red.

Another notable exception was the Border city of Carlisle – perhaps its proximity to Scotland was at least partially responsible. In spite of Scotland's alleged penchant for socialism and for being more 'community minded' than England (that is, at least, the view of the MacChattering classes), outside the four cities, this country was much more 'company' than 'corporation' territory when it came to the operation of local buses.

Of the provincial burghs that had operated municipal tramways only two, Kilmarnock and Perth, survived as bus operators and both of these were gone by 1934. Paisley, the largest town in Scotland, was never a municipal bus operator, nor did the council operate trams either. However, local bus services in Paisley and district had an individual feel due to the presence of several local private operators, such as Cunningham's and Graham's. Municipal transport never took shape in Hamilton, Motherwell, Coatbridge and Airdrie, all located in the densely-populated, coal and steel-making belt immediately east and south-east of Glasgow. Had these towns been in Lancashire, rather than Lanarkshire, they almost certainly would have run corporation buses, although for many years the twin towns of Airdrie and Coatbridge did enjoy a highly identifiable local service from Baxters Buses.

Given that South Wales was such a municipal stronghold it comes of something of a surprise to learn that Swansea – the Principality's second largest town (and now, city) – was another location that never saw corporation buses.

MISSING MUNICIPALS

In tramway days the local authority owned the track but operation of the services was left to a local company. On tramway abandonment in 1936 the company – by now much enlarged as South Wales Transport – signed a deal with the corporation, allowing the former to operate local bus services for the next 21 years. The agreement also contained a provision permitting Swansea Corporation to take over and operate the services at the end of it, and in 1956 there was a strong opinion among a large body of councillors that this should be enacted. However, the desire for corporation buses later waned and Swansea remained outside the loop.

Belfast was the only operator of corporation buses in Northern Ireland but the Province almost had a second undertaking in Londonderry/Derry, which ran its own trams until 1928. In anticipation of the closure of the tramway, the city council ordered six single-deck buses as initial replacements but minds changed and these were sold on to a local independent operator the following year and municipal involvement in local transport provision came to an end.

Back on the mainland, the south coast resort of Hastings, though never an operator of municipal buses, also had something of a corporation bus 'feel' as a result of its extensive, privately operated network of trolleybuses which were actually branded 'Hastings Tramways'. Apart from the absence of a coat of arms on the lower side panels, these were virtually indistinguishable from corporation trolleybuses elsewhere. Indeed with their livery of dark (but dignified) green complemented by cream relief, the vehicles were extremely similar to those trolleys operated by Derby Corporation.

THE CORPORATION BUS

At the other end of England, on Tyneside, the buses of Gateshead and District (with branding heavily emphasised on the town name) could have been taken for municipals but for the absence of a coat of arms.

It was back in the south, in Hampshire, however, that one found the greatest example of the corporation bus that never was - King Alfred Motor Services in the ancient city of Winchester.

Wholly privately owned by a local family, and required to operate on commercial lines, this operator nevertheless had the 'look and feel' of a municipal operator – dark green livery with the lower panels carrying a crest depicting King Alfred with the name WINCHESTER below it. In fact to some eyes, King Alfred buses looked more 'municipal' than some genuine municipals!

King Alfred was the brainchild of a local entrepreneur, Robert Chisnell, who launched his first town route in 1920. Further routes, including two circulars, followed and King Alfred quickly became established as the premier local bus company.

By 1945 it was operating 11 services, even though Winchester is a small city and it continued to grow over the next two decades, the service numbers increasing to 20 by 1965.

After that King Alfred started to feel the same financial pain inflicted on its 'real' municipal equivalents but here there was no recourse to the rates to make up any deficit. The company tried to sell out to Winchester City Council who – whatever its feelings on the matter – was precluded from doing so by government legislation. Private interests also failed to respond and in April 1973 the end came for King Alfred – Britain's municipal bus undertaking that never was.

15

1969-1974

The giants come tumbling down

If it is of any compensation to those who rightly regard 1969 as the beginning of the end for the corporation bus, the demise of this institution could, in reality, have begun much, much earlier than it did.

Following its landslide victory in the general election of 1945, the victorious Labour government had actually earmarked municipal transport undertakings for nationalisation. However, for various reasons (principally, the perilous state of the economy) these were eventually left out of the various legislations that brought the railways and coal industry into public ownership and also transferred control of generating stations from local to national government. So, the 'corpies' were given a stay of execution that lasted for at least another 20 years; but Westminster got them in the end.

Labour lost power in 1951 and for the next 13 years of Conservative rule, municipal transport undertakings were more or less left alone as the Tories concentrated on what were considered more pressing issues such as ending rationing and meeting their ambitious targets for new public housing. When, in 1964, Labour was returned to office, it had a parliamentary majority of just four. However, when the Prime Minister, Harold Wilson, went to the country in an audacious snap election in March 1966, he increased the majority to 100, giving the party real power to implement the policies it stood for.

One of these policies was the creation of regional authorities to co-ordinate all passenger transport (rail, bus and, if appropriate, ferries) within the metropolitan areas outside London. However, how much this had to do with creating – or attempting to create – a seamless, integrated system of local public transport in each of these areas is open to debate. Although he had gained the Labour leadership on a clear left-wing ticket, Harold Wilson soon became a pragmatic centrist when he had to deal with the realities of power. It is common for political leaders (of all mainstream parties) to provide sweeteners to help keep their more radical elements in check and in this case there was more than a suspicion that a national integrated transport system, partly owned by the state and partly by newly created giant regional councils, was one of these. In other words, the corporation bus may have become an expendable political pawn.

Consequently, the Transport Bill started to make its way through parliament, finally becoming an Act in October 1968, with a view to implementation within a year.

What the government planned was the setting up of several passenger transport authorities in England, initially on Merseyside, Greater Manchester, the West Midlands and Tyneside, and one, on Clydeside, in Scotland. These bodies – comprised of local elected representatives – would set out transport policies that were region-wide rather than local. Carrying out such policies would be professionally managed passenger transport executives who, on behalf of the authorities, would co-ordinate all forms of public transport within each designated area.

To kick things off, it was intended that the bus fleets of the various municipal operators would be handed over to the new PTE's, with the purchase of other local bus operators (both public and private) being a longer-term aim. Whether or not local rail services would eventually be controlled and operated by the PTE's, or by British Rail as agent of the PTE's, was, for the time being, left up in the air.

Understandably, opposition among the municipalities was fierce, with some of the strongest critics of the government legislation being Labour aldermen and councillors. Although resistance to change is a natural phenomenon, even when it is for the better, in this case the arguments in favour of the status quo seemed perfectly valid. Although the glory days of the 1950's had gone, not all corporation undertakings were struggling and a drain on the rates. And even when an undertaking required rates support, what the ratepayers got in return was the benefit of a bus timetable (especially out of peak hours) that few private companies could possibly have provided on a strictly commercial basis.

Critics also warned of the financial consequences of bringing a number of municipal undertakings, varying greatly in size, under the one umbrella. For example, differences in scale were reflected in the wage structure, with the big city bus systems paying more per hour than the smaller, peripheral authorities, where the job of crews was reckoned to be less stressful. The Bill's opponents claimed that the Government's plans were highly inflationary because when everyone was answerable to the same employer – as the proposed passenger transport executives would become - the trade unions would demand that crews receive the same rates of pay across the organisation, with the highest paid becoming the benchmark for everyone. To this they might have added additional costs incurred by, among others: the legal change of title, the acquisition and fitting out of plush new city centre offices, hiring of public relations and various other sundry consultants. All of this came to pass.

Others protested on the grounds of "if something ain't broke, why fix it?" The Manchester and Birmingham conurbations, the Government was told, already enjoyed a good level of co-ordination through joint services operated by the various local municipal operators, which made the cost of creating a new body to carry out a similar function highly questionable. On The Wirral side of the River Mersey there was already substantial co-ordination between Birkenhead and Wallasey corporations, a significant number of whose services were timed to coincide with the ferries and nationalised commuter trains linking the Wirral peninsula with Liverpool.

Some critics also doubted if full integration and co-ordination could ever be possible anyway if the municipal fleets were the only ones to be forcibly absorbed by the new PTE's, leaving other operators (nationalised and privately owned) beyond their control. Others questioned how committed a jealously independent British Rail would be to the local passenger transport authorities.

More abstractly, but nevertheless of extreme relevance, were the objections relating to the loss of civic pride, which would be an inevitable consequence of the new set up. For many councils, the ability to operate their own bus network was a badge of honour, and this filtered down to the ordinary citizen, who, it was argued, would be further alienated from public transport if it were provided by an anonymous and distantly managed 'board'. In the Manchester area the name chosen for the new authority was SELNEC, a somewhat clumsy and bureaucratic acronym for 'South East Lancs, North East Cheshire'. Thus Bolton Corporation Transport, for example, would simply become part of something called 'SELNEC North' and local buses would no longer carry Bolton branding, livery or the town's coat of arms. The great city of Manchester itself, along with its smaller but fiercely independent-minded neighbour, Salford, was to be cloaked in anonymity under the operating title of 'SELNEC Central'.

To counter these objections, vague promises were made about retaining the various colour schemes of the constituent authorities but the cynics who doubted this were later proved correct when the multi-coloured former municipal buses were eventually given standard PTE branding.

And so, between 1 October and 1 November 1969, 17 municipal undertakings – including the three largest in England – simply disappeared, and without a penny in compensation paid to the local authorities whose buses and other infrastructure were taken from them.

On 1 January 1970, the new Tyneside PTE absorbed the undertakings of Newcastle and South Shields, with Sunderland following in 1972, after which the organisation became Tyne & Wear PTE.

Tyneside was, perhaps, the strangest case for a PTA and PTE of all in England. There were only two municipal fleets, Newcastle and South Shields, meaning that most of the bus operators in the area would not – at least for the first few years – would not come under the wing of the PTE. And although the council providing the largest fleet – Newcastle – was under Conservative control, when membership of the PTA was drawn up, it did not contain one Conservative member.

Across the Border, the Greater Glasgow (later, Strathclyde) PTE took over the operations of Glasgow Corporation Transport in the spring of 1973. Local government reorganisation in England, effective from 1 April 1974, coincided with the launch of the West Yorkshire and South Yorkshire PTE's, an event that signalled the end of the corporation transport undertakings of Leeds, Bradford, Huddersfield, Halifax, Sheffield, Rotherham and Doncaster. On the other side of the Pennines, the same reorganisation saw Wigan absorbed by SELNEC (which soon became Greater Manchester) and St Helens and Southport by Merseyside PTE, the fate of the latter causing outrage among the local citizenry who wanted their own district status within Lancashire (truncated as the Palatinate was by then) – a move that would have kept Southport buses under local ownership and control. At the same time, Coventry was absorbed into the new West Midlands metropolitan county, and as a result its corporation buses were transferred to West Midlands PTE which had absorbed the fleets of Birmingham, Wolverhampton, Walsall and West Bromwich more than four years previously.

Reorganisation of local government in Scotland, one year later, led to the Edinburgh, Dundee and Aberdeen fleets losing their traditional city names (and crests) in favour of the new regional titles of Lothian, Tayside and Grampian – despite the fact that their service operations never became anything remotely 'regional' and few, if any, local people identified with the new authorities, despite large sums of public money spent on propaganda to get them to do so.

Slowly but inexorably, the link – both real and abstract – between local people and *their* local buses was being eroded.

16

Beyond 1986

Picked off, one by one

Despite the ravages of the previous decade, by the end of the 1970's there were 49 bus undertakings still in municipal ownership in Great Britain.

The biggest surviving fleets belonged to cities that that had not been 'metropolitanised' as part of the reorganisation of local government; these included Nottingham, Leicester, Southampton, Hull, Cardiff, Plymouth and Portsmouth. The word 'corporation' no longer graced the sides of buses but some authorities simply changed the branding from 'corporation transport' to 'city transport', and the coat of arms remained in common use, although that ubiquitous phenomenon, the logo gradually became more popular with operators.

Still, some of the survivors did lose their old identity – e.g. 'East Staffordshire District Council' had much less of a ring to it than its predecessor, 'Burton Corporation', and were Swindon people really happy to see their town name replaced on local buses by something called 'Thamesdown'?

The largest survivor of all was Edinburgh but because of different local government changes in Scotland (where transport became a regional responsibility) the undertaking was now called Lothian Region Transport, although the network pattern remained much the same as it had done in the days of Edinburgh Corporation Transport.

After losing power in 1974, the Conservatives were returned to office in 1979 and even though the new Prime Minister, Margaret Thatcher, was already well known for her free market economic policies, there ensued a fairly lengthy armistice between central government and what remained of local municipal transport. However that lasted only until the Iron Lady first saw off General Gaultieri in the South Atlantic and then, closer to home, Arthur Scargill in South Yorkshire. Then she (and her transport secretary, Nicholas Ridley), began setting their sights on the bus operating industry. The result, in 1985, was another Transport Act, which was implemented the following year.

In a complete reversal of Labour policy, the latest Act provided for the opening up of bus operations to competition, including those in the metropolitan counties, where integration and co-ordination had been painfully slow. Initially, there was optimism in some quarters that deregulation within the metropolitan areas would see bus operation returned to local, district council control, possibly leading to a revival of Rochdale blue and white, Wolverhampton green and Stockport red. Such hopes were, however, short lived as it soon became apparent that this Transport Act was as much about paving the way for bus privatisation as encouraging bus competition – although the new regime had plenty of critics among Conservative councillors just as the (Labour) Transport Act of 1968 had not been

THE CORPORATION BUS

well received by many of that party's representatives in local government.

In theory, however, the provisions of the Act did set the sort of scenario of which many an old-time corporation transport manager must have dreamed. Under the legislation local authorities were allowed to retain their transport undertakings but as arm's length companies, operating on a purely commercial basis. Socially necessary, but unprofitable, services were still permitted but the financial responsibility for this lay with the council and not its 'private' bus undertaking. Thus at long last municipal managers were freed from the political interference that had dogged so many of their predecessors.

Also, the new Act abolished monopoly areas and operators were given the power to launch a bus service, wherever they wished, simply by giving 42 days' notice to the relevant licensing authority. This meant that the council companies were no longer constrained by their own municipal boundaries and were thus in a position to extend services to expanding outlying areas of population without lengthy and costly legal wrangling.

Unfortunately this cut both ways because it enabled the growing private companies that had begun to emerge under the Tories to compete with the municipalities on what was described as a level playing field. In strictly legal terms, yes, the playing field was level and not before time, according to critics of municipal protectionism. However the playing field soon became decidedly unlevel because many of the council owned companies simply proved to be no match for the predatory instincts of their business-savvy commercial rivals. Thus, by the beginning of the 1990's the remaining municipals were starting to bite the dust with depressing regularity. In some cases the councils were made an offer by a corporate rival that they felt they couldn't refuse; in others the municipal bus-operating arm simply collapsed and any remaining assets were sold off. Several councils tried to maintain local ownership by encouraging an employee buyout scheme. However these too began to fall by the wayside after fairly short periods, with the worker-shareholders – and who can blame them in the circumstances? – influenced by one-off payouts and promises of relative job security and an improved career structure under the umbrella of a national corporate organisation.

A milestone was reached in 2009 when the pioneering Eastbourne undertaking was sold to Stagecoach, despite some years earlier having opened its doors to a French minority shareholder, Keolis, a subsidiary of the French national railway operator, SCNF. At the end of that year Plymouth, one of the largest of the remaining survivors, was sold to the Go-Ahead group, despite a trade union campaign against the sale managing to sign up 25,000 names in a petition (roughly 10 per cent of the entire population of the city). However, some comfort could be taken from the fact that the new owner had a policy of maintaining local branding and identity (e.g. Brighton and Hove). The year ended in a double whammy with the impending sale of Islwyn Borough Transport (formerly West Monmouthshire UDC – a long time favourite with bus enthusiasts) to Stagecoach. And just as this title was about to go to press, in early 2010, talks had begun between Ipswich Buses and Go-Ahead relating to a part-sale of the latter's undertaking.

Meanwhile, also in 2009, Preston Bus, the last surviving municipal employee buyout, threw in the towel – also to Stagecoach, although the Competition

Commission then intervened and ordered the new owner to sell on Preston Bus.

Consequently, at the time of writing there were less than a dozen municipal bus companies left in Britain: Lothian (formerly Edinburgh), Blackpool, Rossendale (the 1968 amalgamation of Rawtenstall and Haslingden), Halton (formerly Widnes), Warrington, Nottingham, Ipswich, Reading, Thamesdown (formerly Swindon), Cardiff and Newport.

What is particularly sad about some of the sell-offs is that the municipal bus companies were not underperforming, either financially or in terms of passenger service, although it has to be said that the return on turnover acceptable to a council was significantly lower than would be expected by the shareholders of a purely private operator. Rather, some councillors saw them as a disposable asset to be sold for some pet project such as a museum or sports centre or simply to help reduce council debt.

So if current trends continue it is possible that by the end of 2019, half a century on from that first mortal wounding of the corporation bus, all the municipal undertakings in existence at that time may have gone, despite the fact that a few of the survivors have been recent winners of the 'Best Bus Company in Britain' award and have won plaudits for innovation.

But does the complete demise of municipal transport mean that a particularly important ethos of corporation bus has to disappear also?

Since the late 1980's, cities and towns up and down the country have, at various times, been marking the centenary of the birth of municipal transport in their respective areas. Invariably, the dominant bus service provider (usually part of one of the big national groups) has joined in the spirit of the occasion by repainting one (or more) of its vehicles in former 'corporation' livery, complete with the town or city fleet name and coat of arms. According to various reports, the appearance of these vehicles has given vent to a wave of nostalgia among middle aged and elderly members of the public (some of whom even believed this was the prelude to a comeback by "our" buses), as well as eliciting keen interest among a younger generation who had never seen a corporation bus or, had they done so, were of such a young age that they could not remember the experience.

This reaction is not in itself evidence of any overwhelming desire for the return of local municipal buses (although the Plymouth petition might hint otherwise), either among the public or even politicians, except perhaps those who oppose private provision of public services for reasons of dogma. Barring some unforeseen political earthquake, the corporation bus, as we remember it, has had its day, no matter how much nostalgically inclined individuals like this author would wish otherwise. Just as the rest of the world has put behind it much loved icons as diverse as Watneys Red Barrel and steam locomotives, so the bus operating industry has moved on too.

Nevertheless, it could be a mistake to dismiss this public sentiment over their 'lost' buses as mere nostalgia. On the contrary, perhaps it provides a strong hint to current bus operators of the potential commercial spin-off from tapping into a branding policy that specifically identifies with local markets. In this the corporation bus truly excelled and it is something its private successors have yet to come close to matching.

17

Preserved for Posterity

Where to catch a vintage 'Corpy'

At the time of writing the number of remaining bus companies in municipal ownership still in Britain was receding rapidly, although the word 'corporation' had long since vanished from their branding and the coats of arms has mostly been replaced by that ubiquitous latter day form of identity, the 'logo'.

Fortunately, it is still possible to catch a 'real' corporation bus as examples of the genre exist in museums up and down the country – and in many places these can be travelled on, and not simply gawped at, during 'running days' that are held at various intervals during spring, summer and autumn.

Unsurprisingly, given the intensity of corporation bus activity within a ten-mile radius of its centre, one of the largest collections of municipal buses in the country is to be found at Manchester, where the Museum of Transport is owned by Greater Manchester PTE and operated by Greater Manchester Transport Society. The huge collection boasts 17 buses operated by Manchester Corporation alone, nine from Stockport, and four from Salford. Bolton, Wigan, Bury, Rochdale, Oldham,

Leigh, Ramsbottom and Stalybridge are also there. www.gmts.co.uk

The most comprehensive collection of Liverpool Corporation Buses belongs to the Merseyside Transport Trust (www.mttrust.co.uk), the range dating from 1945 to the very last bus delivered to Liverpool Corporation in 1969. Although the collection (which includes several other operators) is kept in storage in a location not open to the general public, examples can often be seen at rallies and other events of interest to the enthusiast.

Across the Mersey, Birkenhead, Wallasey and Chester corporation buses are represented at the Wirral Transport Museum, Birkenhead (www.wirraltransportmuseum.org) while no less than 11 buses in Blackpool livery and a further nine in that of Lytham St Annes/Fylde are owned by the Lancastrian Transport Trust, which is based in Blackpool (www.ltt.org.uk).

The North West Museum of Road Transport in St Helens is another municipal hotspot, housing several buses from its home town plus examples from Widnes, Warrington, Leigh, Lancaster, Southport, Chester, Preston, and Darwen. (www.hallstreetdepot.co.uk)

Corporation buses of the West Midlands abound at The Transport Museum, Wythall, near Birmingham (just off jct 3 of the M42), which boasts no less than 13 vehicles that entered service with Birmingham City Transport between 1913 and 1968. There are also four Walsall vehicles, three from Wolverhampton (including a trolleybus), two from West Bromwich and one from Coventry. www.thetransportmuseum.org.uk

There is also some municipal representation at Aston Manor Road Transport Museum within Birmingham itself. One of the highlights of the year here is the Outer Circle Running Day, during which visitors are transported by vintage bus along part of Birmingham City Transport's famous No11 Outer Circle route. www.amrtm.org. As might be expected, Coventry Corporation is well represented at the Museum of British Road Transport in the city. www.transsport-museum.com

Two museums give splendid examples of corporation buses that operated outside the big conurbations. Ipswich Transport Museum (www.ipswichtransportmuseum.co.uk) boasts corporation trolleybuses as well as motorbuses while Lincoln Corporation is well represented at the Lincolnshire Vintage Vehicle Society (www.lvvs.org.uk)

In Yorkshire there is a strong Leeds and Bradford representation at Keighley Bus Museum (www.kbmt.org.uk) but perhaps pride of place goes to a Straker-Clough trackless (i.e. trolleybus) dating from 1924. Currently on loan to the museum, this was introduced into service by Keighly Corporation, which unfortunately folded as a municipal bus operator before world war two. South Yorkshire Transport Museum (formerly Sheffield Bus Museum) at Rotherham has a strong Sheffield representation in addition to buses from the municipal fleets of Rotherham, Rochdale and Leicester. www.sytm.co.uk

The premier attraction north of the Border is the Scottish Vintage Bus Museum at Lathalmond, near Dunfermline. www.busweb.co.uk/svbm Aberdeen, Dundee, Edinburgh and Glasgow corporations are all represented here, the latter by one of that city's first double-deckers. But there are also several English municipal buses on show, including one from Middlesbrough, the only operator to retain route lettering for the entire lifetime of the undertaking. Limited opening is available at Bridgeton Bus Garage (www.gvvt.co.uk) where the Glasgow Vehicle Vintage Trust currently has three Glasgow Corporation vehicles (including a single deck trolleybus) in store, prior to Glasgow City Council's first class Transport Museum being moved to new premises. Across the water, Ulster Folk and Transport Museum (www.uftm.org.uk) at Cultra, Co Down, boasts a motorbus and trolleybus from Belfast Corporation.

Perhaps the best museums of all are the 'living' variety, and for the municipal bus enthusiast, pride of place probably goes to the Trolleybus Museum (www.sandtoft.org.uk) at Sandtoft, near Doncaster. Most of the trolleybuses here were municipally owned and many of the former operators, from Glasgow in the north to Reading in the south, are represented. There is also a fleet of motorbuses, with Douglas and Grimsby among the corporation examples on show. The museum boasts a large circuit of overhead wiring, enabling the trolleybuses to be operated on various open days throughout the year. These are often themed events, such as a weekend devoted to six- wheel (i.e. three-axle trolleybuses) or twilight running when trolleybuses – with sparks flying in the enclosing darkness - are perhaps at their most impressive.

The East Anglia Museum of Transport (www.eamt.org.uk) at Lowestoft also boasts a large collection of municipal trolleybuses, including examples from Derby, Belfast, Bournemouth and Manchester. Not surprisingly, given the location, the motorbus collection includes several buses from the former Lowestoft fleet as well as from nearby Great Yarmouth.

Several municipal trolleybuses operate under the wires at the Black Country Living Museum in Dudley, Worcestershire (www.bclm.co.uk) as does a Newcastle Corporation trolleybuses at the North of England Open Air Museum at Beamish, Co Durham. www.beamish.org.uk

Readers should check with the various websites for full details of opening times, running days and other special events.

Bibliography

In compiling this book, reference has been made to the following publications. Many of these are still in print and are recommended for detailed reading on various individual municipal operators

Accrington's Public Transport, Robert Rush; Landy Publishing, 1986

Belfast Corporation Transport, W.M. Montgomery; Colourpoint Books, 2001

Blackpool's Buses, David Dougill; Transport Publishing Company,1982

Birmingham City Transport, Malcolm Keeley; Ian Allan, 2005

Brighton Trolleybuses, (Trolleybus Classics Series); Middleton Press

Bolton Corporation Transport (Super Prestige), Harry Postlethwaite; Venture Publications, 2007

Buses of Sunderland Corporation Transport (The), Mel Kirtley; 1993

Bournemouth Transport, Colin Morris; Ian Allan, 2003

Bournemouth Trolleybuses (Trolleybus Classics Series); Middleton Press

Bradford Trolleybuses, (Trolleybus Classics Series); Middleton Press,

Cardiff Trolleybuses (Trolleybus Classics Series); Middleton Press

Characters of the Bus Industry; Omnibus Society, 2004

Derby Trolleybuses (Trolleybus Classics Series); Middleton Press

Derby City Transport Route History, B.K. Edwards and J.G. Simpson; Omnibus Society, 1983

THE CORPORATION BUS

Edinburgh's Transport: The Corporation Years, DLG Hunter

Exeter, A Century of Public Transport, R. C, Sambourne; Glasney Press

Grimsby/Cleethorpes Trolleybuses (Trolleybus Classics Series), Middleton Press

Golden Age of Tramways (The), Charles F Klapper; David & Charles

History of British Bus Services – North-east (A), David Holding; David & Charles, 1979

History of British Bus Services – South Wales, David Holding and Tony Moyes; Ian Allan, 1986

History of the British Trolleybus (A), Nicholas Owen; David & Charles, 1975

Huddersfield Trolleybuses (Trolleybus Classics Series); Middleton Press

Hull (Super Prestige), John Banks, Venture Publications, 2003

Hull Trolleybuses (Trolleybus Classics Series); Middleton Press

Ipswich Trolleybuses (Trolleybus Classics Series); Middleton Press

Last Tram (The), Charles Oakley; Glasgow Corporation, 1962

Leeds Transport Vol 4, J Soper; Leeds Transport Historical Society, 2007

Liverpool's Buses, Paul Kelly; Transport Publishing Company, 1986

Local Transport in St Helens, T.B. Maund and J. J. Ashton; Venture Publications, 1995

Maidstone Trolleybuses (Trolleybus Classics Series); Middleton Press

Manchester & Salford, A Century of Public Transport, Michael Eyre and Chris Heaps; Ian Allan, 2000

Middlesbrough & Stockton (Prestige Series), Philip Battersby; Venture Publications, 2002

Municipal Buses in Colour, 1959-74; Reg Wilson; Ian Allan, 1997

Nannying, Bradford Trolleys and Buses, 1960-75; S. Ledgard, Bobtail Press, 2007

BIBLIOGRAPHY

Newcastle Trolleybuses (Trolleybus Classics Series); Middleton Press

Nottingham 2 (Prestige Series), John Banks; Venture Publications, 2002

The Oldham Bus Scene, 1945-1969, Jim Wild, 1970

On The Buses (West Bromwich), Harry Rees; Kithead Ltd, 1995

Plymouth, 100 Years of Street Transport, R. C. Sambourne; Glasney Press

Preserved Municipal Buses, John A Senior; Venture Publications, 1996

Preston's Trams and Buses, Mike Rhodes; Venture Publications, 1985

PSV Circle fleet histories: Cardiff and Newport, 1980

PSV Circle fleet histories: St Helens and Southport, 1989.

Reading Transport, Colin Morris, Ian Allan, 2005

Reading Trolleybuses (Trolleybus Classics Series); Middleton Press

Scottish Municipal Operators, Gavin Booth; Ian Allan, 1990

Sheffield (Super Prestige Series), Philip Battersby; Venture Publications, 2002

South Shields Transport, John Carlson and Neil Mortson; Tempus Publishing, 2007

Streets of Cardiff, Roger Davies; Ian Allan

Trolleybus Trails, J Joyce; Ian Allan, 1963

Trolleybuses of Newcastle upon Tyne (The), T.O. Canneaux and N.H Hansen; Newcastle upon Tyne City Libraries, 1985

Twighlight Years of the Trams in Aberdeen and Dundee, Alan Brotchie; Adam Gordon

Wallasey Bus (The), T B Maund; Boumphery, 1995

Wolverhampton Trolleybuses (Trolleybus Classics Series); Middleton Press

Official brochures and reports

75 Years of Public Transport in Burton upon Trent, Peter Bowles; East Staffordshire District Council, 1973

Coventry Transport, 1912-1974; City of Coventry, 1974

History of Manchester's Tramways (A); Manchester Corporation, 1949

Halifax Passenger Transport, 1898-1968; Halifax Corporation, 1968

Lancaster City Transport, 75 Years; Lancaster City Council, 1978

Fifty Years of Motorbuses, Leicester City Transport; 1974

Newcastle upon Tyne City Transport Undertaking, 1901-69; Newcastle City Libraries, 1969

Report on the Future Operation of Municipal Transport in Glasgow (A), E.R.L Fitzpayne; Glasgow Corporation, 1948

100 Years of Southampton Transport; City of Southampton, 1973

Timetables, etc

Aberdeen Corporation Transport Department, 1965

Birkenhead Municipal Transport, 1960

Borough of Chesterfield Transport Department, 1973

Liverpool Corporation Passenger Transport, 1960

Manchester Corporation Transport Services, 1960

'Sheffield Telegraph' Railway and Motorbus Guide, 1962

Magazines

Buses; Buses Illustrated; The Classic Bus

Websites

Peter Gould's website provides a feast of information on many municipal transport undertakings, particularly in relation to their embryonic stages, www.petergould.co.uk

Other relevant websites with informative history sections are:

Barrow Transport, http://website.lineone.net/~barrow_transport

Birmingham Corporation Buses (Peter Walker – Birmingham History Forum), http://forum.birminghamhistory.co.uk

Blackburn Transport Net http://homepage.ntlworld.com/duncan.holden46/buses/busindex.htm

Brighton & Hove, http://www.buses.co.uk

Burnley Colne & Nelson Society, http://myweb.tiscali.co.uk/bcnsociety/bcnjtc.htm

Colchester Bus History, http://www.aspects.net/~markcol/colbus/

Dundee Corporation Transport, http://www.skylineaviation.co.uk/buses/dundee.html

Eastbourne double- and single-deckers, http://www.skylineaviation.co.uk/buses/ebrnedd.html

Friends of King Alfred Buses, www.fokab.org.uk

Halton Borough Transport, http://www.haltontransport.co.uk

Huddersfield Passenger Transport Group, www.jsh1949.co.uk

Hull Corporation Transport (Paul Morfitt), http://www.freewebs.com/hullpaul

Ian Semple (Glasgow Transport) www.semple.biz

Ipswich Transport Museum, http://www.ipswichtransportmuseum.co.uk

Mike's Bus Pages, www.mikesbuspages.com

Nottingham City Transport, http://www.nctx.co.uk

SCT'61 (Southend Corporation Transport), www.sct.org.uk

Southern Municipals, http://www.regent9.ic24.net/

Thamesdown Transport Limited, http://www.thamesdown-transport.co.uk

Trinity High (Northampton Corporation Transport) www.trinityhigh.co.uk/transport

Warrington Borough Transport, http://www.warringtonboroughtransport.co.uk

Index

Aberdare UDC Transport, 154; Aberdeen Corporation Transport, 168; Accrington Corporation Transport, 86; Accrington Stanley FC, 86; Airdrie, 204; Aldershot 187; Anfield Stadium 41; Armstrong, Gilbert 6; Arriva, 48; Ashton-under-Lyne Corporation Transport, 70; Aston Manor Road Transport Museum, 221; Austin, William 15

Baker, Albert, 178; Baker, Arthur, 178; Baker, Percival, 6; Barnsley 187; Baroth, Charles, 61; Badgerline, 101; Barrow-in-Furness Corporation Transport, 74; Baxters Buses, 204; Bedwas & Machen UDC Transport, 155; Beeching, Dr Richard, 60; Belfast Corporation Transport, 171; Bennett Ralph, 63; Birkenhead Municipal Transport, 48; Birmingham City Transport, 25; Black Country Living Museum, 224; Blackburn Corporation Transport, 84; Blackpool Corporation Transport, 79; Blue Bus Services (Luton), 139; Blue Bus Services (Newcastle), 92; Bluebird Services, 20; Bolton Corporation Transport, 62; Bootle 41; Bournemouth Corporation Transport, 9; Bradford City Transport, 116; Bridgeton Bus Garage, 223; Brighton Blue Bus, 5; Brighton Corporation Transport, 3; Brighton Hove & District, 5; Bristol, 201; British Rail, 209; Burnley, Colne and Nelson Joint Transport Committee, 88; Burrows, Albert, 178; Burton on Trent Corporation Transport 34; Bury Corporation Transport, 65

Caerphilly UDC Transport, 155; Calderdale Joint Omnibus Committee, 122; Cardiff Corporation Transport, 147; Carlisle, 204; Chandler, Richard, 145; Chester City Transport, 52; Chesterfield Corporation Transport, 140; Chisnell, Robert, 206; Chrysler, 37; Cleveland Transit, 98; Coatbridge, 204; Colchester Corporation Transport, 22; Colwyn Bay Corporation, 157; Comfort Coaches, 137; Competition Commission, 217; Cooper, John, 141; Coventry Corporation Transport, 35; Cox, R. Edgeley, 31; Cox, Ronald, 180;

INDEX

Crossville, 48; Cunningham, Ian, 11; Cunningham's Bus Services, 204; Cunuder, Felix, 149

Darlington Corporation Transport, 100; Dartmoor, 12; Darwen Corporation Transport, 86; Deakin, Edward, 107; Derby Corporation Transport, 138; Devon General, 14; Doncaster, Corporation Transport, 126; Douglas Corporation Transport, 173; Dundee Corporation Transport, 166

East Anglia Museum of Transport, 223; East Lancs Regiment, 86; East Staffordshire District Council, 214; East Yorkshire Motor Services, 127; Eastbourne Corporation Transport, 1; Eastern Counties, 144; Eastern National, 20; Edinburgh City Transport, 164; England, Ben, 133; England, Harry, 179; Eston UDC, 104; European Cup, 132; Exeter Corporation Transport, 14

Fearnley, Arthur, 179; Fearnley, Ronald, 179; Federation of Municipal Transport Employers, 27; Fielden, JA, 141; Fitzpayne, Eric, 179; Fitzpayne, Frederick, 179; Franklin, Joseph, 181; Fylde Borough, 81

Gaultieri, (General) Leopoldo, 215; Gelligaer UDC Transport, 156; Glasgow Corporation Transport, 159; Gloucester, 202; Go-Ahead Group, 217; Goodison Park, 41; Graham's Bus Services, 204; Grampian Region, 213; Grampian Transport Holdings, 142; Great Western Railway, 16; Great Yarmouth Corporation Transport, 142; Greater Glasgow/Strathclyde PTE, 212; Greater Manchester Transport Society, 220; Grimsby/Cleethorpes Transport, 129

Halton Transport, 218; Halifax Passenger Transport, 120; Halifax JOC, 120; Hamilton (Lanarkshire), 204; Hants & Dorset Omnibuses, 7; Harding, G.G., 183; Hartlepool Corporation Transport, 98; Haslingden Corporation Transport, 89; Hastings Tramways, 205; Hilditch, Geoffrey, 182; Huddersfield Corporation Transport, 118; Huddersfield Town FC, 120; Humpidge, Chaceley T, 106; Hyde, Derek, 182

Imperial Chemical Company, 99; Ipswich Corporation Transport, 145; Ipswich Transport Museum, 222; Institution of Electrical Engineering, 175; Isle of Man National Transport, 174; Islwyn Borough Transport, 217

Jackson, C.J. 12

Keighley, 88; Keighley Bus Museum, 222; Keolis 217; King Alfred Motor Services, 206; Kingston upon Hull Corporation Transport, 127; Kilmarnock, 204; Kirklees Council, 120

Lake District, 74; Lancaster City Transport, 77; Lancashire United Transport, 46; Lancastrian Transport Trust, 221; Leeds City Transport, 104; Leicester City Transport, 135; Leigh Corporation Transport, 64; Lincoln Corporation Transport, 130; Lincolnshire Vintage Vehicle Society, 222; Liverpool Corporation Passenger Transport, 38; Llandudno UDC, 158; Lloyd Kohler, 53; London General Omnibus Company, 143; London Transport, 19; Londonderry/Derry, 205; Lord, Thomas, 178; Lothian Region 213; Lowestoft Corporation Transport 143; Luff, Walter, 80; Luton Corporation Transport, 19; Lytham St Annes Corporation Transport, 81; Lythgoe, Frank, 103

Maidstone Corporation Transport, 23; Manchester Corporation Transport, 56; Manchester City FC, 57; Manchester Utd FC, 57; 'Mancunian' (The), 59; Mansfield, 187; Marks, W.G., 39; Marples, Ernest, 185; Mersey Tunnel, 40; Mersey Railway Company, 48; Merseyside PTE, 212; Merseyside Transport Trust, 220; Merthyr Tydfil Corporation Transport 152; Mexborough & Swinton Traction Company, 124; Midland Red, 25; Middlesbrough Corporation Transport, 102; Ministry of Transport, 106; Morecambe & Heysham Corporation Transport, 75; Morton, Norman, 95; Motherwell, 204

National Bus Group, 187; Naughton, Michael, 185; New Brighton, 50; Neal, Albert, 181; Newcastle upon Tyne City Transport, 90; Newport Corporation Transport, 150; North of England Open Air Museum, 224; North Western Road Car Company, 54; Northampton Corporation Transport, 141; Northern Bluebird, 189; Northern General Transport Company, 95; North West Museum of Road Transport, 221; Norwich, 203; Nottingham City Transport, 132; Notts & Derby Traction Company, 133

Oldham Corporation Transport, 69

Paisley, 204; Partick Thistle FC, 163; Perth, 204; Pilcher, R Stuart, 57; Plymouth City Transport, 11; Pontypridd UDC Transport, 153; Poole, 10; Portsmouth City Transport, 7; Potteries Motor Traction

INDEX

Company, 203; Preston Corporation Transport, 82; Preston Bus, 84; Pulfrey, George, 128

Ramsbottom UDC Transport, 66; Rawtenstall Corporation Motors, 89; Reading, 17; Red & White, Motor Services, 157; Ribble Motor Services; 41; Ridley, Nicholas, 215; Rochdale Corporation Transport, 66; Rossendale Transport, 218; Rotherham Corporation Transport, 124; Rugby, 203

Salford City Transport, 60; Scargill, Arthur 215; Scarborough, 203; Scottish Bus Group, 187; Scottish Vintage Bus Museum, 222; SELNEC, 211; Sheffield JOC, 124; Sheffield Transport, 121; Silvers, Charles Owen, 29; Smith, Ernest, 185; SMT, Eastern and Midland, 162; South Notts Bus Company, 135; South Staffordshire Tramways Company, 33; South Wales Transport, 205; South Yorkshire PTE, 212; South Yorkshire Transport Museum, 222; Southdown Motor Services, 8; Southampton Corporation Transport, 5; Southend-on-Sea Corporation Transport, 21; Southport Corporation Transport, 46; South Shields Corporation Transport, 93; Stafford, 203; Stafford, Charles, 88; Stagecoach 217; Stormont Building, 173; St Helens Corporation Transport, 42; SHMD, 54; Stockport Corporation Transport, 53; Stockton on Tees Corporation Transport, 99; Stoke on Trent, 203; Stokes, (Sir) Donald, 181; Stokes, Harry, 181; Sunderland Corporation Transport, 95; Sussex Downs, 4; Swansea, 205; Swindon Corporation Transport,16

Tayside Region, 213; Taylor, Frank, 198; Taylor, Harry 69; Tees-side RTB, 104; Thamesdown Council, 17; Thatcher, Margaret, 215; Todmorden JOC, 121; Torquay, 14; Train, George Francis, 48; Transport Act 1968, 208; Transport Act 1985, 215; Transport Museum, Wythall (The), 221; Trent Motor Traction, 139; Trolleybus Museum, Sandtoft, 223; Trotter, Neville, 90; Tyneside/Tyne & Wear PTE, 211

Union Jack Omnibus Services, 20; Ulster Folk and Transport Museum, 223; United Automobile Services, 91; United Counties, 20

Vickers shipyard, 75

Wakefield 203; Wallasey Corporation Motors, 50; Walsall Corporation Transport, 30; Warrington Corporation Transport, 45;

Warwick, Dionne 199; Watneys Red Barrel, 219; Waveney Council, 144; West Bridgford UDC Transport, 134; West Bromwich Corporation Transport, 32; West Hartlepool Corporation Transport, 97; West Midlands PTE, 212; West Monmouthshire UDC Transport, 155; West Riding Automobile Company, 106; West Yorkshire PTE, 107; Westcliff Motor Services 21; Western National, 12; Western Welsh, 157; Widnes Corporation Transport, 44; Wigan Corporation Transport, 71; Wirral Transport Museum, 221; Winchester, 206; Wilson, Harold, 208; Wolverhampton Corporation Transport, 28; Woolton Omnibus Company, 38; Worcester, 204

XL Motor Services, 20

Yellow Buses, 11; Yom Kippur War, 198; Yorkshire Traction, 101